#LIVESENT

LIVE SENT

Equipping You To
Conversations In E

RYAN FONTENOT

FOREWORD BY SHANE PRUITT

For more information, email office@rageministries.com
ISBN: (paperback) 979-8-88759-497-2
ISBN: (ebook) 979-8-88759-498-9

This book is dedicated to the love of my life, Heather. Outside of Jesus, no human has had more influence on my life than you. Honestly, this book would not even exist if it were not for your continual belief in and encouragement to "write the book." Thank you for being you. I am a better man, the world is a better place, and eternity is being impacted because of you.

I'm so excited you are taking this journey with me. I would like to offer you a free Video Summary of each chapter to help guide you along the way. To get your exclusive access, just head on over to my website today.

www.livesentbook.com/videos

Together #WeAreRAGE

Ryan

Foreword

One of the most important things I learned as a student pastor and local church pastor is that whatever we celebrated the most as a ministry is what we were intentionally or unintentionally teaching our people to believe is what was most important. So the principle is "celebrate what you want to replicate"!

If we're saying that evangelism, discipleship, and living on mission are most important, then that is what we should be celebrating most frequently. So, if reaching people with the Gospel is extremely important, we should be intentionally celebrating when souls are reached with the Gospel! One of the best ways to celebrate this is to teach people what the Gospel is, train them how to articulate the Gospel, and equip them to be on mission. Simply put, we must empower people to ***live sent!***

Think about it – we've all heard the stats concerning the Next Generation of young people. Here are some sobering ones. According to a poll that we took through my Twitter account asking people, "*at what age did they surrender to Jesus Christ as Lord and Savior of their life?*" 2,694 people answered the poll, and we found that 77% of all the born-again Christians that responded surrendered to Jesus before the age of 18 years old. And 95% of all Christians surrendered to Jesus before the age of 30 years old. Let that sink in for a moment. That is why evangelism, in particular to the next generation, is so essential. Of course, I believe that God can save people at any age. He does it every day. However, practically speaking, if we don't reach people during those "student and young adult years," we lose a whole generation. So there has to be an urgency to this.

I honestly believe the most effective person in reaching a college student or teenager with the Gospel is another college student or teenager with a heart that beats with passion for Jesus. And that same heart is broken over the spiritual lostness of their generation. If students are Christians with the Holy Spirit, they are not the church's future; they are the church right now. So, we must "equip the saints for ministry" to know Jesus and make Jesus known. Sometimes, those saints are teenagers and college students. Students sharing the Gospel is often just as much for the believer as for the unbeliever. Students diligently evangelizing their friends is a highly effective form of discipleship.

That is why this book by my friend, Ryan Fontenot, is so essential. When he asked me to write the *Forward*, I did not hesitate for a second to jump at the opportunity to be a part of this. This book is timely, relevant, and a much-needed help to shift the paradigm. Let's reach people with the Gospel. Let's impact the generations for the glory of God. Let's ***live sent***!

So, it begs the question, "How do you do that?"

Hopefully, asking that question led you to pick up this book. There is no one better leader than Ryan to write this book. It is not theory for him; it is practice. He does it, he lives it, and he can teach others to do the same thing. So let my friend, Ryan, help you navigate how to ***live sent*** and how to equip others to do the same!

Shane Pruitt
National Next Gen Director
North American Mission Board – NAMB
Author of the books: *9 Common Lies Christians Believe* and *Calling Out the Called*
@shane_pruitt78

Table of Contents

Introduction

I was the youngest brother growing up. On many weekends at our house, there would be me, my older brother, my older stepbrother, and often some of their friends. Needless to say, I always wanted to fit in and do what they were doing.

Growing up in East Texas, we had tons of woods, which provided a new adventure each and every day. Finding trails, hunting toads, killing snakes … you name it, and we probably did it in those woods. One of the things I stood in awe of early on, though, was when my brothers would "ride trees." If you have no idea what that is … hang on!

The woods of East Texas are often called the "Piney Woods" because of the pine trees that cover them. Pine trees are soft and flexible and actually make an incredible tree to "ride." The general idea of tree riding is to find a tree, climb up the tree, get high enough until the tree starts bending, grab hold with your hands, let go with your feet and literally ride the tree all the way to the ground. The slow, gentle descent is amazing … in theory.

One day, my brother thought it was time for me to experience this adventure as well. So off to the woods we went, in search of the perfect tree for me to conquer. Finally, after a few minutes of searching, looking, and inspecting, we found "the tree."

After a few seconds of instruction and with a little of their encouragement (insert sarcastic brotherly challenge here), I began to scamper up the sapling.

My initial ascent was probably no more than five feet off the ground. For me, it seemed much higher than when I was on the ground watching. Already my hands began to sweat. "Is this high enough?" I asked nervously.

"No!" my brother yelled back, "Keep going!"

I moved up the tree five more feet. Now, at about ten feet up, I felt the tree swaying a bit … or maybe it was just my body beginning to shake. "Is this high enough?" I asked once more.

"No, keep going!" I heard once more.

With great hesitation, I inched my way up another five feet or so. Surely this was it. The tree swayed even more, and my body clung even tighter to the poor sapling. "Now!?"

But no, I was not nearly far enough up, according to my brother. "Keep going, keep going!" they screamed. Despite everything in me saying "don't," I kept going.

Not wanting to disappoint and trusting my brother for some unknown reason, I climbed another five feet, trembling all the way. Sure enough, the tree swayed even further back and forth at this point. I was sure I was far enough now!

"Is this good?" I yelled down.

Finally, I heard the words I wanted to hear from below, "Yes, that's it! Just let your feet go now!" It was the time I had waited for. It was a moment I dreamed of. Finally, it was time to let go and "ride the tree!"

Truth be told, I would never have learned to ride a tree and feel the exhilaration of the free fall to the ground if my brothers would not have been there with me. I wouldn't have dared go at this alone. I would have stayed with my feet firmly planted on the ground, safe, secure, and unscathed.

I am writing this book because I believe this is exactly how many of us are living our Christian life right now—safe, secure, and silent about our faith. Living in silence about Jesus leaves us wondering, isn't there more to this Christian life? We were not made to be silent. We were made to shine and share Jesus in this world. Charles Spurgeon once said, "To be a soul winner is the happiest thing in the world. And with every soul you bring to Jesus Christ, you seem to get a new heaven here upon earth."

My hope is that I could be a sort of "big brother" for you. I want to cheer you on, give you clarity, provide you with the steps necessary, and be here to tell you to "keep going" when everything in you says to stop. No, I don't want to train you to climb trees; I want to help you climb *mountains*. Like thousands of others I have trained over the past two decades, I want to help you experience the joy of living on the mission Jesus saved you to walk in. I want to be part of seeing you not merely know Jesus and walk with Jesus … but live a life that is unafraid to share Jesus with others.

This journey will not be easy. At times, everything in you will say, "That is far enough; I can't go any higher." Your body will cling to the safety of silence. But together, and with the help of the Holy Spirit, I believe you will step into a life on a mission that you have never known possible, or only seen others experience.

Together we will climb the tree. Together we will experience the ride of a lifetime by learning to let go of fear and cling to Jesus in order to live a life that is unafraid to tell others about the hope found only in Him.

When I finally let go of that tree with my legs that day, I experienced something I never could from the ground. I believe, by God's grace, we will learn to let go of our fears and excuses and experience the ride of a lifetime as we learn to #LiveSent and tell our world about Jesus.

CHAPTER 1

The World "Out There" and the Problem "In Here"

> "After that whole generation had been gathered to their fathers, another generation grew up, who knew neither the Lord nor what he had done for Israel."
>
> Judges 2:10 NIV84

"How much do you have to hate somebody to not proselytize? How much do you have to hate somebody to believe that everlasting life is possible and not tell them that?"

–Penn Jillette

One of my favorite sports to play growing up was football. From as far back as I can remember, I have always loved playing, watching, and just being part of the game. Don't hate me here, and I might lose some readers right now, but I am a diehard Dallas Cowboys fan. But you have to remember; I did grow up in their glory days! So cut me a little slack, at least.

The thing about football, and really, any sport, is this: to get better, you have to focus. To learn the fundamentals, you have to focus. To learn the plays, you have to focus. To fulfill your job on the field, you have to focus. Even if you're in the stands and you are a fan, you have to focus.

Focus is the key in so much of life. Whether that be sports, work, family, or health, you name it; if you want to get better and excel, you have to get into focus. The same is true if you want to #LiveSent. You have to begin focusing. You have to understand the reality. You have to see the big picture. So let's begin with a glimpse of why you, committing to living a #LiveSent life, matters so much.

There are nearly 7.3 billion people in the world today. Of those 7.3 billion people, it is estimated that 31 percent claim to be followers of Jesus.[1] That is about a third of the global population. This may sound great, but this is just the tip of the iceberg.

Of the global population, it is estimated that 1.3 billion are adolescents (age 10–19). At the time of this writing, teens make up 11 percent of the global population.[2] However, there are some truly alarming findings in recent surveys among the next generation. Of those in Generation Z (born 1996–2012), nearly 34 percent in the United States claim to be atheist, agnostic, or have no religious affiliation at all.[3] As well, only 4 percent of Gen Zers hold to a biblical worldview.

Just over 40 percent of teens globally identify as Christian.[4] Among those who do claim to be Christ-followers, we are seeing some alarming stats as well. Over half of teens identifying as Christian believe all religions teach equally valid truths.[5] Two out of every five teens who identify as Christian say they never read their Bible.[6]

There is actually a piece of really good news amongst global teens, though. Two in three teens indicate that their spiritual journey is important to their life.[7] What does this mean for us, you ask? It means that while there is a vast number of teens around the globe who do not yet know Jesus, the majority of students are seeking some spiritual answers. This means … opportunity! They are open to having conversations; they are open to invitations; they are open. So what is the real problem, then, you ask?

If I'm going to be gut-level honest at the very start of the book, the problem is not the people who *do not* know Jesus; the problem is the people who *do* know Jesus. It's not the people "out there"; it is the people "in here."

Sharing Our Faith Is Both Our Delight and Our Duty

One of the truths that broke my heart when reading some of these findings is that "44 percent of Christian teens disagree that they even have a responsibility to share their faith with others."[8] We are literally losing a generation because we have failed to help this generation of Christ followers realize the joy of sharing Jesus with others.

Adults do not fare much better. Most adults who claim to follow Jesus have told no one about Jesus in the past six months.[9] As a result, we have a generation of people who claim to be followers of Jesus who are missing out on one of the greatest honors in their journey with Jesus: telling others about Him.

In neglecting this one aspect of the Christian life—personal evangelism—we are missing out on one of life's biggest blessings. A former mentor of mine once said (and I hold this to be true in my life also), "Apart from my family and me personally coming to Jesus, there is no greater joy than getting to share the hope of Jesus with someone who does not yet know Him."

How many people in your life do you know who do not know Jesus right now? And how many of them have you ever taken the time to share the Good News of Jesus with them? I want you to picture the thrill of seeing your lost friend, your lost family member, your lost classmate come to life in a relationship with Jesus. This is the hope we have. This is the opportunity before us.

But we need to understand the problem is not out there. The problem is not with those who do not know Jesus—the problem, or might I say *the solution,* is with those of us who do know Jesus getting intentional about sharing Him with others.

I wrote this book to bring into focus the reality that is before us. If we don't take the call to go and tell our world about Jesus seriously, we will continue to lose a generation. Evangelism has to rise to the top of our hearts once again in the life of every Christian. No, I am not talking about you or me "saving" anyone. John Stott wrote, "To 'evangelize' … does not mean to win converts … but only to announce the Good News, irrespective of the results."

This is the call on our life. Jesus said, "Follow me, and I will make you fishers of men." To tell the world of the only One who can save them is both the delight and duty of every follower of Jesus!

The World Needs Jesus

The Bible describes a world in desperate need of Jesus. Judges 2:10 speaks of a generation that grew up and "did not know the Lord nor the things He had done." That type of generation, an endangered generation, is, once again, right before our eyes. As followers of Jesus, you and I are called to take the message of Jesus to our world, where we are with who we know. You and I were not called to reach the entire world, but we are called to reach *our world.*

Jesus took twelve ordinary men and flipped the known world upside down. He turned fishers into followers, tax collectors into truth-tellers, persecutors into preachers, and murderers into missionaries. Jesus has always used the unexpected to do the unexplainable.

Today, I believe Jesus wants to do the same with you. As you journey through this book, I believe you will sense the Spirit of God work in and on you in ways you never thought possible. You are going to realize one of the main calls God has on your life: to let the world know about Him.

If we are going to be serious about seeing the world come to Jesus, we each need to get serious about telling those *in our world* about Jesus. We have to *focus* and realize the ***lostness*** of our generation and the ***responsibility*** we all play in getting the news of Jesus to them.

No longer can we just rely on Sunday services or event evangelism to win our friends. Trust me; these have their place for sure. But today, we have the opportunity to become as passionate, equipped, and willing to open our own mouths and share our stories, our lives, and the gospel with the world around us. It's time for you and me to step into our calling to #LiveSent!

#LiveSent Reflections: Take 5 minutes to answer these questions below.

1. What did the Holy Spirit say to you, and what stood out to you the most?
2. What scripture came to mind or spoke the loudest to you as you read?
3. What is one next step you can take today in light of what you just read?
4. Who do you know that needs to hear what you just learned in this chapter?

#LiveSent Challenge: Take time each day to ask God to help you get rid of the excuses holding you back and ignite a fire in you to tell people in your life about Jesus.

CHAPTER 2

The "Why" Behind the "What"

"But in your hearts, honor Christ the Lord as holy, always being prepared to make a defense to anyone who asks you for a reason for the hope that is in you; yet do it with gentleness and respect."

1 Peter 3:15

"When your WHY is clear, the HOW becomes easy."

–Unknown

Why? Generation Z has become known as the "Why Generation." Although I believe each generation, and each person for that matter, truly wants to know *why*, but this is especially true for the next generation.

Forbes wrote of the "Why Generation" like this …

> In the classroom, at the workplace, it's the question every young person is asking today. Why do we need to do it this way? Why is this important? Why can't we try doing it differently?
>
> This can be frustrating for parents, educators, employers, and others in the older generations who interact daily with Millennials and Generation-Z. Though this constant question can feel like a delay tactic, disrespect, or even insubordination, in general, nothing could be further from reality.
>
> The Why Generation is not asking why in order to stall, show off, or flout authority. Their constant "Why?" is an honest question. They need to know the background information so they can forge a new

> path forward. Because they've been raised to believe they are unique, special, and important, they care about making their mark on whatever they are involved in. Many times when they ask why, what they're really asking is if a better way exists.[10]

I, too, like to know "Why?" and I believe you need to know the answer to "Why?" as well. "Why does this even matter?" When it comes to the area of evangelism and sharing Jesus with others, why should we #LiveSent? Why must you personally get serious about telling people about Jesus? Why is it so important for us to share our faith with the world around us? The "why" matters.

Billy Graham, the most famous evangelist of all time, said it like this, "One of the greatest priorities of the church today is to mobilize the laity [the everyday follower of Jesus] to do the work of evangelism." You see, Billy Graham was a real "Good News" teller. He traveled the globe, speaking to millions of people in stadiums packed all across the planet. But Billy Graham knew the greatest priority of the church is the greatest need of the church. That is, for every follower of Jesus to be trained to share their faith with *their* world. He knew the greatest way to reach the world is to get every believer equipped and active, competent, and confident in sharing their faith with others.

Paul would write in Romans 10:15, "How are they to preach unless they are sent? How beautiful are the feet of those who preach the gospel?" The truth is, if you are in

Christ, you are sent. I like to say it like this, "Saved people are sent people." Unfortunately, though, the majority of believers who claim to follow Jesus aren't *really* following Jesus. A recent global youth survey discovered that "4 out of 10 Christian teens don't believe they have a responsibility to share their faith with others."[11]

S.D. Trueblood said, "Evangelism is not a professional job for a few trained men, but it is instead the unrelenting responsibility of every person who belongs to the company of Jesus." If one of the greatest priorities of the church is to equip the body to tell the world about Jesus, yet the overwhelming majority of those who claim to follow Jesus, aren't doing this—Houston, we have a problem.

I honestly believe, though, it boils down to a "Why?" problem for many of us. Believers just need to know "why." They honestly want to know, "Why does this matter? Why should I #LiveSent? Why is this so vital? Why does this matter so much?" You just need to know why. So I want to quickly share with you a few reasons behind you and I beginning to go and tell.

#1 Why: Because God Loves the World

Everything Jesus did was driven out of love. His love for the Father and His love for others. So too, our number one "Why" for telling others about Jesus ought to be *love*. The Apostle Paul wrote in 1 Corinthians 13 this powerful reminder, "If I speak in the tongues of men and of angels, but have not love, I am only a resounding gong or a clanging cymbal." Don't miss this.

Our driving force for sharing Christ in this world ought to be our deep love for God and genuine love for others. When we realize how much Jesus has rescued us from, we will more regularly share with others how they can be rescued as well. Grasping each day what we have been saved for empowers us to open up our mouths and share the hope of Jesus with others.

God loves you. God loves me. God loves the world. "For God so loved the world, that he gave his only Son, that whoever believes in him should not perish but have eternal life" (John 3:16). It is the daily reminder of this unthinkable love of God that will propel us to make Jesus known to others.

#2 Why: Because God Said So

Living sent is vital because it is a command from our Father in heaven. God the Father commanded us to go and tell, Jesus the son commanded us to go and tell, and the Holy Spirit empowers us to go and tell. In Matthew, in His final words to His disciples, Jesus said, "Go therefore and make disciples of all nations, baptizing them in the name of the father and of the son and of the holy spirit, teaching them to observe all that I've commanded you and behold I'm with you always to the end of the age" (Matthew 28:19–20).

Jesus said that we are to make disciples. And if we are going to make disciples, we know that all disciples begin with *decisions*. Yes, decisions aren't the end, but they are the *beginning*. There is no disciple of Jesus who has not first made a decision to follow Jesus.

As well, Jesus would say in Mark 16:15, "Go into all the world and proclaim the gospel to the whole creation." In other words, it is the command given from God the Father, through God the Son and empowered by God the Holy Spirit, for us to go and open up our mouths to everyone everywhere all the time and tell them about Jesus.

In John 20:21, Jesus, again, would say, "Peace, be with you. As the father has sent me, now I am sending you." Did you see that? Jesus is now sending ***you.*** The question then is, what did Jesus send us *to?* The Father sent Jesus to "seek and save the lost." And now you and I are to be about letting the lost know there is a Jesus who's come to seek and save them. If that's the business He was about, it's the business we should be about as well.

Luke 24:47 would record these words of Jesus, "repentance for the forgiveness of sins should be proclaimed in his name to all nations, beginning from Jerusalem." So God's plan from the beginning is that you and I would go and tell the world about Jesus. It would start in Jerusalem and spread all over the world. And we would talk about repentance and forgiveness of sins that is available only in Christ.

Finally, let me say that in Acts 1:8, we see the role of the Holy Spirit. The Bible says, "But you will receive power when the Holy Spirit has come upon you, and you will be my witnesses in Jerusalem and in all Judea and Samaria and to the ends of the earth." You and I have been commanded to go by the Father through the Son, and we now have power with the Holy Spirit to fulfill this go-sent life.

So why should we go and tell? Because it's commanded by our heavenly Father—or quite plainly: because God said so!

#3 Why: Because People in Hell Are Begging

A third answer to "Why?" is the hell-sentenced sinner cries for it. Let me show you, then talk about it. In Luke 16, we have an interesting story recorded of the rich man and Lazarus. The rich man dies and goes to Hades, and Lazarus goes to heaven. We see a plea from the rich man for a drop of water to be given to quench his thirst. Once he is told this cannot happen, listen to his next request ...

> "He answered, 'Then I beg you, father, send Lazarus to my father's house, for I have five brothers. Let him warn them so that they will not also come to this place of torment'" (Luke 16:27–28, NIV84).

So here we see the rich man in hell being tormented, and his one last pleading was for God to send someone to his brothers so they would not come to this place. I believe with all my heart every soul in hell right now would tell you and me, as Christ-followers, "Go tell someone about Jesus!" Live your life to tell the world about everlasting life found only in Christ. Do all you can to tell all you can about Jesus.

Charles Spurgeon said it best, "Oh, my brothers and sisters in Christ, if sinners will be damned, at least let them leap to hell over our bodies; and if they will perish, let them perish with our arms about their knees, imploring them to stay, and not madly to destroy themselves. If hell must be filled, at least let it be filled in the teeth of our exertions, and let not one go there unwarned and unprayed for."

You and I are to be about telling the world about Jesus. We hear it commanded by God, but we also hear the plea from those who have rejected Christ and have died. They do not want anyone to join them in hell. And so you and I have the incredible responsibility to be about this one task of telling those we know about Jesus. As Carl Henry said about the gospel, "The gospel is only good news if it gets there in time."

#4 Why: Because People Everywhere Are Looking

Let me now give you one final, "Why?". We must go and tell because there is a harvest waiting to be won. There are souls waiting to trust Jesus. There are people looking for hope, and they're not just across the globe. Many are just across the room.

They are in your locker rooms, in your lunchrooms, in your classrooms, and in your house. They are in your neighborhood. They are at your job. They are everywhere. People are looking, longing for hope. They know this world is messed up; they know something has gone terribly wrong. The Bible reminds us of that hope and that hope has a name; His name is Jesus.

In John 4:35, Jesus would warn, "Do you not say, 'Four months more and then the harvest'? I tell you, open your eyes and look at the fields! They are ripe for harvest" (John 4:35, NIV84).

Jesus was imploring his followers to not wait any longer. He didn't want them to wait another day. Today is the day to tell others about Him. The reason our ministry, R.A.G.E. Ministries, is aimed primarily and predominantly at the next generation is because of what research has clearly shown us.

A Barna study revealed that nearly two out of three born-again Christians (64 percent) made their commitment before their eighteenth birthday.[12] That means if we do not get them before they turn the tassel, if they haven't bowed the knee before they grab the diploma, it is very likely they never will.

And so we want to not just preach or proclaim Jesus to the next generation; we also want to prepare you to do the same. That is why I have undertaken the task of writing this book. That is why ***you*** are reading it right now. To become ***confident, competent***, and ***consistent*** in sharing Jesus with your world, right where you are.

You and I need to be about this business. We need to be prepared. The love of God compels us. The Lord has commanded it. Those in hell are crying out for you to do it. And a harvest of souls is waiting for you to share with them.

T. L. Osborn once said, "One way, Jesus. One job, evangelism." Students, youth, pastors, moms, dads, and whoever might be reading this book, today is the day to get prepared.

Today is the day to take your faith seriously. Today is the day to stop asking ***why*** and take a step toward learning ***how.***

#LiveSent Reflections: Take 5 minutes to answer these questions below.

1. What did the Holy Spirit say to you, and what stood out to you the most?
2. What scripture came to mind or spoke the loudest to you as you read?
3. What is one next step you can take today in light of what you just read?
4. Who do you know that needs to hear what you just learned about in this chapter?

#LiveSent Challenge: This week, pick out one of the verses shared in this chapter, write it down on a sticky note and commit it to memory.

CHAPTER 3

You Need Power

"After they prayed, the place where they were meeting was shaken. And they were all filled with the Holy Spirit and spoke the word of God boldly."

Acts 4:31

"The great people of the earth today are the people who pray, (not) those who talk about prayer."

–S.D.Gordon

The other night, my family and I were all gathered upstairs to watch a movie. Everything was ready: popcorn, snacks, and drinks. We had it all and were ready for an epic family movie night. Suddenly, the room went completely dark, the TV turns off, and we sit there in complete darkness. No lights, no TV, nothing but utter darkness. Needless to say, our kids let out a scream for the ages! Our house had officially lost power.

If you want to have light, you need to have power! If you want to live a life that declares Jesus to those around them, you need power. Jesus said, "I am the light of the world." Later, Jesus would look at His disciples and tell them, "You are the light of the world." For there to be light, power is a non-negotiable.

We have a saying around the R.A.G.E. Ministries team, "Prayer is the power." We believe that when we pray, God does what only God can do. When we pray, God also gives us supernatural power from the Holy Spirit to do what we have been called to do. In order for us to be people that regularly declare Jesus to others, we have to be filled with the power of the Holy Spirit. This power is found in prayer. Prayer is where Jesus found His power; prayer is where the early church found power in the Holy Spirit, and it is where we will find our power daily as well. I penned this definition of prayer one day as a reminder for myself. "Prayer is the unable and incapable calling out to the almighty and more than able." This definition came to me after reading Ephesians 3:20–21 one day:

> "Now to him who is able to do far more abundantly than all that we ask or think, according to the power at work within us, to him be glory in the church and in Christ Jesus throughout all generations, forever and ever. Amen."

These verses reminded me of two amazing truths. First, God is more than able to do whatever we ask or even think. Think about that; no pun intended. The Lord tells us you can do more than we can ever ask; He is literally ***more than able***.

Second, I was reminded that I am absolutely unable to save anyone. Salvation is of the Lord, from the Lord, to the Lord, through the Lord, and for the Lord. I get to be a part, but I do not save anyone. If we want to see people saved in our life, we have to consistently call out to the only one who can save.

Samuel Chadwick once wrote, *"The one concern of the devil is to keep the saints from prayer. He fears nothing from prayerless studies, prayerless work, prayerless religion. He laughs at our toil, mocks at our wisdom, but trembles when we pray. Prayer turns ordinary mortals into men of power ... It brings fire. It brings rain. It brings life. It brings God. There is no power like that of prevailing prayer."* If the devil can keep us from prayer, He will keep us from the power.

Prayer changes things. Prayer changes us. Evangelism is first worked in our hearts before it is worked out of our mouths. So, let's look at seven specific prayers that will fill us continually with the power of the Holy Spirit and empower us to #LiveSent.

1. Pray for a Heart for God

If we want our life to be lived for Jesus, and for Jesus to be known all of our lives, our first prayer is for God to give us a heart for Jesus. In Mark 12:30, Jesus says the greatest commandment is to *"Love the Lord your God with all your heart, all your soul, all your mind, and all your strength."* Don't miss this! Our greatest commandment from God is to love God. We are to daily ask God daily to give us a deep abiding love for Jesus.

God is more interested in *you* than He is in what you can do for Him. God wants you to know Him. He wants to be known by you before you go to make Him known to others. And the more we know Him, the better we will represent Him. So seek the Lord with all your heart. Seek first the kingdom of God and His righteousness. Our first priority is to be our daily walk and relationship with Jesus.

2. Pray for a Heart for Others

The second prayer we need to begin to practice is a prayer for God to give us love for other people. I've often heard people say, "I love God; I just don't love people." While statements like these have a bit of humor to them, if we are not careful, we will actually begin to live these jokes out.

It is true, people, relationships, friendships, family, coworkers, peers, teammates, teachers, neighbors, and everyone else can be very difficult in life. We are all sinners, and thus we are all difficult to get along with. So we need to ask God not only to give us a deep love for Jesus, but also for others.

Right after declaring the first and greatest commandment, Jesus quickly gives us the second: "And the second is like it; you shall love your neighbor as yourself." Jesus wanted to make sure that his hearers not only sensed a call to love God, but also realized that their love for God is to drive them out to love others. We should continually ask God daily to give us a genuine love for all people, in all places, at all times.

3. Pray for God to Give You Open Doors

We all go to different places every single day. We go to work, school, practice, grocery stores, the neighbor's house, the mailbox; we go all over every single day. As we go, we need to ask God to give us open doors of opportunities to tell other people about Jesus.

This is the prayer that Paul prayed in Colossians 4:3 when he said, "At the same time, pray also for us, that God may open to us a door for the word, to declare the mystery of Christ, on account of which I am in prison." I am always amazed when I read this verse in Colossians. I am amazed because Paul was in prison, and he was asking God to give him an opportunity—not to be released, but to tell others about Jesus.

Is this how we see our life? Is this how we see our job? Is this how we see our school? Is this how we see our family? Is this how we see our neighborhood? Are we too busy praying to "get out" that we miss the opportunity to speak out? Instead of feeling trapped, frustrated, and imprisoned, let's see them as opportunities to tell people who don't know Jesus about Him.

As you go about your day, ask God to open up your eyes daily as you go, to those around you who are in need of Jesus so that you might open up your mouth and tell them about Him.

4. Pray for Open Hearts to Hear

Have you ever been talking to someone only to realize everything you were telling them just wasn't quite registering with them? It's like, no matter how hard you try to explain something to them, they are just not getting it.

When it comes to sharing the gospel with somebody, the Bible tells us God is the one who opens their hearts to hear. There is a clear example of this recording for us in Acts 16:14. The Bible records, "One who heard us was a woman named Lydia, from the city of Thyatira, a seller of purple goods, who was a worshiper of God. The Lord opened her heart to pay attention to what was said by Paul."

Did you see what the Bible says? "The Lord opened her heart to pay attention." It's very clear that Lydia understood the message Paul shared because God had opened her heart. We need to be a people who are praying for God to bring us to people and that He would open their hearts to understand the gospel message. We need to ask God to open blinded eyes, deaf ears, and closed hearts.

When we pray for God to open hearts, we are asking God to do something that we are absolutely unable to do, but He is more than able to do.

5. Pray for Personal Boldness

"Pray also for me, that words may be given to me in opening my mouth boldly to proclaim the mystery of the gospel, for which I am an ambassador in chains, that I may declare it boldly, as I ought to speak" (Ephesians 6:19–20, ESV). In this prayer, we see one of the boldest men ever to live for Jesus, asking the church to pray for him to have boldness. We cannot underestimate the importance of this prayer. Why did Paul have so much boldness? *Because he prayed for boldness.*

This prayer is one that we all need to pray. Talking to others about Jesus is spiritual warfare. If we do not ask God to give us a spirit of boldness, we will never open our mouths and tell anyone about Jesus. But if we commit daily to asking God for a spirit of boldness, I believe we will be bolder than we could ever imagine.

Make it a habit each day to ask the Lord to give you a spirit of boldness. Open up your mouth and tell someone about Jesus.

6. Pray for Specific People in Your Life

Mark Batterson once wrote, "God does not answer vague prayers. The more specific your prayers are, the more glory God receives" (*The Circle Maker*).[13]

How many times in our prayer life do we just lift up generic, non-specific, and habitual prayers?

"God, bless Monday. God, give us a good day. God, use me today. Thank you for all your blessings." While all of those prayers are okay, none of them are specific. How do we know if God ever answers any of those prayers?

When we pray specifically, we give God the opportunity to *answer* specifically. I saw this happen during one of our weekend retreats where I was speaking. At the beginning of our time together, I asked the leaders to pray specifically for kids by name. Many of the leaders took my challenge.

One youth pastor specifically listed three students they were asking God to save that weekend. On Saturday night, all three of those guys came to Jesus! He prayed specifically and saw God answer specifically. Needless to say, that leader's prayer life has changed forever.

When you and I have a list of people we are specifically praying for, we put God in a position to show off. We give God a path to increase our faith by answering those prayers. So, who in your life specifically needs Jesus? Is there one person, two people, or a whole list? Get specific, make a list, and start praying!

When we pray specific prayers, God will answer specifically.

7. Pray for More People to #LiveSent

As a final prayer for us to be praying, I want us to pray what Jesus said to pray. I want us to pray for God to send out more workers into the fields. Jesus said it like this, "The harvest is wonderful, but the laborers are few. Ask therefore the Lord of the harvest to send out laborers into the harvest field."[14]

This is a direct command from Jesus on something that we ought to be praying for. Asking God to raise people to go and tell others about Jesus should be a regular prayer of our life. There are people without Christ everywhere we go. In every domain of our world, someone needs to know Christ. We only need to ask God to send people there and empower them to declare.

When we ask God to send out others, we will be sent out as well. God works in our hearts as we pray for Him to work in others' hearts.

In Jeremiah 33:3, we find one of the most powerful promises of prayer found in scripture. The Lord says, "Call me, and I will answer you and show you great and mighty things you do not know." Don't miss this promise from God. When we pray, we will see God do great and mighty things that we had no idea God could do. When we pray, we see God not just work somewhere else through someone else, but work right here, right now, every day. Let's pray because prayer is the *power.*

#LiveSent Reflections: Take 5 minutes to answer these questions below.

1. What did the Holy Spirit say to you, and what stood out to you the most?
2. What scripture came to mind or spoke the loudest to you as you read?
3. What is one next step you can take today in light of what you just read?
4. Who do you know that needs to hear what you just learned about in this chapter?

#LiveSent Challenge: Take these seven prayers, write one each day on your calendar, and set a specific time to pray that prayer. Put these daily repeatable prayers on your calendar and see what God does as you make this a daily spiritual discipline of your life.

CHAPTER 4

What Is This "Good News" You Are Talking About?

"I am not ashamed of the gospel because it is the power of God for the salvation of everyone who believes: first for the Jew, then for the Gentile."

Romans 1:16, NIV84

"The Good News was, and is, that all this has happened in and through Jesus; that one day it will happen, completely and utterly, to all creation; and that we humans, every single one of us, whoever we are, can be caught up in that transformation here and now."

–N. T. Wright

One day, I went to my wife and shared one of the biggest goals the Lord has ever given me. Excitedly, I went to her and said, "Heather, I wanna share with you something I believe the Lord wants us to try to accomplish by 2030. I believe we are to try to train one million students around the globe to share the gospel by 2030." (Check out www.1MillionSent.com.)

Heather looks back at me in all her wisdom and love and replies, "How do you plan to do that?"

I looked back at Heather and said, "I have no idea. What do you think?"

You see, my wife is a planner. She is a strategist. She is gifted in the realm of determining how things can and should get done, and the processes we ought to follow. On the other hand, I am a "Let's wake up and make it happen" type of guy. I am not a naturally gifted planner. Planning is actually hard work for me. I would rather be and live spur-of-the-moment than plan out every single hour of the day. What I found out, thankfully, from the gift God has given me in my wife, is that planning actually is beneficial. As my wife would say, "Prior planning prevents poor performance. It's the five P's, Ryan." When it comes to sharing your faith, there are five P's as well: "Prior Planning Prevents Poor *Proclaiming*." Many people cite one of the main reasons they do not share their faith as much as they would like to is because they do not know what to say. If you and I will actually prepare, get ready, study, and know how to present the gospel, we will experience more gospel conversations than if we were not ready.

While we know the Lord can use anyone who is a believer anywhere at any time to tell anyone about Jesus because evangelism is the work of God—it is spiritual work, a supernatural endeavor—the Lord also encourages us to be prepared. The Bible tells us to "be ready" to give a reason for the hope we have when we're asked. So we are to be ready, and we are to be ***prepared***. In this chapter, we will discover the foundation every believer needs in order to be ready to share Jesus with others. Let's get **prepared**!

The Gospel Defined

Because we are called to share the "gospel," we need first to know what the gospel actually is. Chelsea Kight would say it like this when it comes to the gospel, "The gospel is so simple that a child can comprehend it yet so profound that you will spend a lifetime exploring and experiencing its fullness." So let's start with a quick definition of the gospel.

The word "gospel" is derived from the Old English "god-spel," which means "good news." In the New Testament of the Bible, the gospel refers to the good news of salvation through Jesus Christ. The four Gospels of Matthew, Mark, Luke, and John are included in the Bible and tell the story of Jesus' ***life***, ***death***, and ***resurrection***.

The Apostle Paul would summarize it like this:

> "Now, brothers, I want to remind you of the gospel I preached to you, which you received and on which you have taken your stand. By this gospel, you are saved if you hold firmly to the word I preached to you. Otherwise, you have believed in vain. For what I received I passed on to you as of first importance: that Christ died for our sins according to the scriptures, that he was buried, that he was raised on the third day according to the scriptures, and that he appeared to Peter, and then to the Twelve. After that, he appeared to more than five hundred of the brothers at the same time, most of whom are still living, though some have fallen asleep. Then he appeared to James, then to all the apostles" (1 Corinthians 15:1–7, NIV84).

I really like the way Dr. Rice Broocks, author of God's Not Dead, defines the gospel: *"The gospel is the good news that God became man in Jesus Christ. He lived the life we should have lived and died the death we should have died—in our place. Three days later, He rose from the dead, proving that He is the Son of God and offering the gift of salvation to those who repent and believe in Him" (Man, Myth, Messiah – Answering History's Greatest Question).*[15]

The Gospel Outlined ...

Now that we have a good definition of what the "Good News" is, let's now look at a simple flow or outline of that news. The reason we want you to know the flow of the gospel is so that you can communicate the Good News at any time to anyone, anywhere.

I believe one of the easiest outlines of the gospel message can be summarized in four phrases:

- Salvation Needed.
- Salvation Provided.
- Salvation Accepted.
- Salvation Demonstrated.

Let's take a little time to lay the foundation for us moving forward. When you grasp these four big categories, I believe you are set up not just to have gospel "presentations" but have everyday gospel "conversations." If you can get these four phrases in your mind, you can easily weave the gospel into any conversation at any time.

Salvation Needed

Let's begin with this truth. We all need to be saved. You see, we were created by God to be with God. God made us, loves us, and wants us. But there is a problem: sin has separated us from God.

We were created to have a relationship with God, but because of sin, that relationship was broken. Sin is anything that goes against God's will. It can be something as small as lying or something as big as murder. Sin has consequences, and the biggest consequence is separation from God.[16]

Salvation Provided

Yes, sin has separated us from God. That is indeed bad news. But there is good news! Even though we have sinned and are separated from God, He loves us and wants to restore our relationship with Him. The only way to restore a right relationship with God is through Jesus Christ. Jesus died on the cross and rose again so that our sins could be forgiven and we could be reconciled to God. While we were running from God, God came running for us in Jesus.[17]

Salvation Accepted

We see the bad news; sin has separated us from God, who wants a relationship with us. Then we see the Good News, Jesus came to pay for our sins and bring us back to God. Now we see how a necessary response to the gift offered in Jesus.

The price has been paid, and the gift is available, but it must be received. We receive salvation by receiving Jesus. We receive Jesus not by works, not by trying harder, but only by faith in the full finished work of Jesus. If you repent of your sins and put your faith in Jesus Christ, you will be saved![18]

Salvation Demonstrated

One of the most neglected realities of the Good News is that those who receive Jesus as Lord of their life will demonstrate that with their life. In Jesus, you were dead; now you are alive. You were separated from God; now you are adopted into the family of God. You were in darkness; now you are in light. You were lost; now you are found.

Everything has changed, and now you and I begin walking in that. When a person becomes a Christian, they experience new life in Christ. This new life is demonstrated in several ways.

First, baptism is an outward sign of the inward change that has taken place. It is a public profession of faith and a symbol of cleansing and new beginnings. Second, Christians are called to fellowship with other believers. They are no longer alone but now have a community of fellow believers to share their journey with. Finally, Christians are called to serve others and share the Good News of Jesus Christ with the world. When we see someone living out these three things, we have great confidence that they have experienced new life in Christ.

I hope this chapter has given you a good grasp of what the gospel is and has helped prepare you to get ready to share it with others. This foundation will be critical for you moving forward with competence and confidence in Sharing Jesus.

Remember, prior planning prevents poor proclaiming.

#LiveSent Reflections: Take 5 minutes to answer these questions below.

1. What did the Holy Spirit say to you, and what stood out to you the most?
2. What scripture came to mind or spoke the loudest to you as you read?
3. What is one next step you can take today in light of what you just read?
4. Who do you know that needs to hear what you just learned about in this chapter?

#LiveSent Challenge: This week, commit to memory Dr. Rice Broock's definition of the gospel and memorize the four big categories of the gospel by writing them down somewhere and sharing them with another believer.

CHAPTER 5

A Picture Is Worth a Thousand Words

"For God so loved the world, that he gave his only Son, that whoever believes in him should not perish but have eternal life."

John 3:16

"Evangelism is not a professional job for a few trained men, but is instead the unrelenting responsibility of every person who belongs to the company of Jesus."

–D. Elton Trueblood

In a conversation one day, famous evangelist D.L. Moody was criticized for the way he was doing evangelism. To this criticism, Moody responded, "It is clear you don't like my way of doing evangelism. You raise some good points. Frankly, I sometimes do not like my way of doing evangelism. *But I like my way of doing it better than your way of not doing it"*.

Evangelism is when you and I share the gospel with others. Leith Anderson wrote, "The simple definition of evangelism: those who know, telling those who don't." In other words, evangelism is you and I, who know Jesus, telling those who don't know Jesus. As we learned in the last chapter, the gospel is the Good News that Jesus came to save us from our sins. It is the message of hope that we can be forgiven and have a relationship with God by faith in Jesus Christ as Lord. When we share the gospel with others, evangelism, we are giving them the opportunity to hear about Jesus and make a decision to follow Him.

If we aren't careful, we can easily get paralyzed when it comes to telling others about Jesus. While there are many fears people identify as to why they do not evangelize, one of the biggest fears is "doing it wrong." The truth is, it can seem difficult to know how to talk about Jesus with other people. You may feel like you don't know enough, or like you might say the wrong thing. But sharing your faith doesn't have to be complicated. I have a very simple way to share Jesus with others. It is so simple and clear that you can start using it today.

In this chapter, I want to help you know what to say and help alleviate your fear of "doing it wrong." If you will commit this simple outline to memory and heart, I believe you will be prepared to begin talking about Jesus with your friends, your family, and anyone else the Lord may bring into your life today. I regularly get stories of people who have shared Jesus with someone for the very first time. Because they learned this presentation, they were able to have their first gospel conversation.

My friend Greg Stier likes to say, "I don't go into a steak restaurant for the plate. I go for the steak. The gospel is the steak that must be presented. The plate is the method through which we present it. Choose your plate and serve the steak." I want to share with you the "plate" I love to serve up the gospel on. So let's get ready to share the Good News of Jesus together.

Check Out These Pics

The old saying goes, "A picture is worth a thousand words." One picture can communicate so much. Since this is true, I believe we can summarize the gospel in four pictures. Or, because it is 2023, how about four emojis?

Let's start by looking at four emojis, four big words, and a good description of each. Understanding this flow will help you have a better understanding of the gospel and an easy way to communicate it to others.

: God

If you ask anyone, anywhere, what the heart represents, they will say "love." The heart is a powerful symbol that is universally recognized. It represents many things, but most importantly, it represents love.

Do you know what the Bible says? It says, "God is love." So while the heart does truly represent love, it ultimately represents God. A restored relationship with God is the greatest need of every human being, and it is only through His love that we can find true fulfillment in life.

: Sin

The division symbol represents sin. Sin started in the Garden of Eden when Adam and Eve sinned against God. Sin is any rebellion against God.

Ever since then, sin has been separating people from God. A good way to describe sin using the division symbol is to explain the horizontal line as sin, with the top dot representing God and the bottom dot representing us. So visually, you can now see sin is the dividing mark between God and us.

The Bible says that we have all sinned and fallen short of the Glory of God. Because of sin, we are separated from God, who made us and desires a relationship with us.

✝ : Jesus

The cross points us to the Good News Himself, Jesus. The wages of sin is death, but because of Jesus Christ, we can have eternal life. The Bible says Jesus is the only way for us to get back to God. The truth is, while we were running from God in rebellion and sin, Jesus came running after us.

Jesus died on the cross for our sins and was resurrected three days later. This is the gospel, and it is the foundation of our faith. Jesus is the only way to know God, and His death and resurrection provide the only way for us to be forgiven and have eternal life.

? : Decision

The question mark reminds us there is a decision that we must make. In other words, what are you going to do with

Jesus? Information alone doesn't bring transformation. Only when we choose to believe and receive Jesus does the Good News take root in our life.

The question is not, "Does God love you?" The question is not, "Does sin separate us from God?" The question is not, "Can Jesus save you?" The *only* question is, "Will you surrender your life to Jesus as Lord?"

The Summary and Scripture

After you have a good grasp on these truths above, I want to provide you with a summary you can memorize and scripture to give you further biblical clarity and understanding.

The flow of this information is not meant to be something you read and repeat to someone else. It is meant to be learned so you can use as much or as little of it as needed when having a gospel conversation with someone.

When I share the gospel with others, I rarely, if ever, drop all of this information. I try to listen for the Holy Spirit's prompting on which portion of each point I need to share. But because I have memorized all of these, they are all at my disposal in sharing the gospel.

♥: **God** – The Bible says God is love.

- ☐ God made you (Psalm 139:13–14).
- ☐ God loves you (John 3:16).
- ☐ God wants you (2 Peter 3:9).

÷: **Sin** – Sin is rebellion from God and His love.

- ☐ Sin infects you (Romans 3:23).

- ☐ Sin separates you (Isaiah 59:2).
- ☐ Sin has killed you (Romans 6:23a).

⊞: **Jesus** – There is hope; His name is Jesus.

- ☐ Jesus came to seek and save you (1 Timothy 1:15).
- ☐ Jesus died on the cross for your sins (Romans 5:8).
- ☐ Jesus rose again to offer you life (Romans 6:23).

? : Decision – What will you do with Jesus?

- ☐ Come to Jesus (Matthew 11:28).
- ☐ Confess Jesus as Lord (Romans 10:9).
- ☐ Call out to Him for salvation (Romans 10:13).

I would challenge you to spend time memorizing the outline above and the scripture that goes along with each one. This is where the work really begins. I promise you, though, the work will be worth it.

The Work Is Worth It

One summer, I was training several hundred students in this very outline. After teaching it to them, I had them practice with others. I shared with them to make sure and be serious about it because the person they are sharing with may not know Jesus.

After a short time of sharing, something amazing happened. We actually saw nearly ten of them lead someone to Jesus. That is the power of the gospel. The Lord used teens who just learned a simple gospel outline to lead another teen to Jesus!

This is what you and I can be part of every day—taking a simple message and sharing it with others in love. Jesus really does change everything!

What an amazing opportunity we have to share the gospel each and every day. When we faithfully tell Jesus' story, lives are changed. People come to know Him as Savior and Lord. This is what Christianity is all about—the Good News that changes everything!

Start learning this outline and then begin having gospel conversations with the people around you. You may be surprised at how God uses you to bring someone new into His kingdom. When we faithfully and continually do this, we become a part of the gospel conversation that leads to gospel salvation.

#LiveSent Reflections: Take 5 minutes to answer these questions below.

1. What did the Holy Spirit say to you, and what stood out to you the most?
2. What scripture came to mind or spoke the loudest to you as you read?
3. What is one next step you can take today in light of what you just read?
4. Who do you know that needs to hear what you just learned about in this chapter?

#LiveSent Challenge: Take time this week to memorize the emojis, what each one stands for, and a good description of each.

BONUS:

As a bonus, we have completely free video training to learn this way to share Jesus. This training can be done alone, or preferably, with a group. Go check out this amazing FREE RESOURCE at www.1millionsent.com.

CHAPTER 6

God Has a Plan to Reach the World

"Declare his glory among the nations, his marvelous works among all the peoples!"

Psalm 96:3

"Everyone likes evangelism, as long as someone else is doing it."

–Ed Stetzer

There is an unusual story recorded for us in 2 Kings of four lepers. Lepers were people who had dreadful and often deadly skin diseases. Those with leprosy would be kicked out of their towns until they either healed or, worse, died. They were literally the untouchables.

While these four men were kicked out of their city, their city was enduring severe famine. They knew if they went back into their city, there would be no food to be had. They knew if they sat where they were, they would soon die. Their only hope was to go to the neighboring city, their enemy's city, in hopes of finding mercy, food, and provision there.

When they arrived at the city near nightfall, there was nobody in the city. The Lord had caused the inhabitants to flee because they heard the sounds of chariots and horses and a great army. Thus, the city was completely empty of people but still full of food, clothing, water, and provisions.

The Bible records next, "The men who had leprosy reached the edge of the camp, entered one of the tents and ate and drank. Then they took silver, gold, and clothes and went off and hid them. They returned and entered another tent and took some things from it and hid them also."[19] A true miracle had happened. They were rescued from certain death and now had more than enough.

As amazing as this rescue truly was, what happens next is even more incredible. In 2 Kings 7:9, the Bible says, "Then they said to each other, "What we're doing is not right. This is a day of ***good news,*** and we are keeping it to ourselves. If we wait until daylight, punishment will overtake us. ***Let's go*** at once and ***report*** this to the royal palace."

This is a powerful picture of the world, you, and me. Apart from Christ, we are all lost, diseased with sin, and headed to certain death. Christ came to earth to provide life. Before Christ, the way was dark, and there was no hope. But Christ came as light into the world and offered life to all who would follow Him.

When we put our trust in Christ, He forgives us of our sins and gives us eternal life. Not only does He give us life, but He gives us life to the full. At the time we received Christ, you and I were saved, healed, cleansed, and adopted into the family of God, never to be the same. Like the lepers who had been rescued, that day was indeed a day of "good news." But unlike the lepers, many of us continue to "keep it to ourselves."

You Are Part of God's Plan

The Lord has a plan. Jesus came to seek and save the lost. He came to set captives free. He came to give life to the full, but people must be told. It is imperative for the good news to be shared.

Right now, I want you to think about:

- People in your life whom I will never speak to.
- Someone in your life who will never show up to your church.
- Someone in your life who will probably never hear a sermon from anyone.
- How many times you talk with these people.

You see, God has put you in their world for a purpose. God has saved you, equipped you, and set you in their sight so that you may both demonstrate the gospel to them and declare the goodness of Jesus to them. ***You are God's plan to get the Good News to them.*** Not me, not your pastor, not your youth pastor, not your small group leader, not a podcast, not a YouTube video, but you are God's plan. And you need to be ready any time, all the time.

A few years ago, I had the joy of going to Ecuador with Samaritan's Purse. We went over there with Operation Christmas Child to hand out shoeboxes to children in villages of great need. It was truly an incredible yet draining experience.

After staying a couple of days in Ecuador, we boarded the plane to head back home. We flew from Ecuador to Atlanta and then from Atlanta to Dallas. When I got on the plane from Atlanta to Dallas, it was late at night, and needless to say, I was pretty exhausted. To be honest, I hoped that I would get a row by myself so I could sleep, rest, recover, and be refreshed by the time I got home.

As people were boarding the plane, I had a row with three seats, and to my surprise, no one was in my aisle. *Yes, my prayers have been answered. I am going to get the rest that I need.* I was pretty excited and had already started settling in for a good two-hour nap.

It seemed like everyone had boarded the plane when suddenly, I saw one final lady hustling onto the plane. She looked frazzled and a bit out of breath. I could tell she had been running really hard to make the flight. I was near the back of the plane, so surely there were plenty of extra seats before she got back to me, but row by row, she edged closer and closer.

I would like to say I was hoping she would come to sit by me, but honestly, I was hoping she would sit down before she reached my aisle. So now I am sitting on the aisle seat of a three-seat row, and sure enough, she stops at my row. Quickly the lady said, "I think this is my row."

I smiled, stood up, and let her have her seat. I was thinking because she was obviously the last person on the plane, she would go ahead and scoot all the way to the window, but no, she sat right in the middle seat. *Are you serious?* I couldn't believe it; I was a little frustrated in my flesh and wasn't quite sure this was what I had planned, hoped, or prayed for.

After a bit of small talk, the plane was ready for takeoff. As much as I wanted to close my eyes and get some rest, I knew something was happening in this lady's life. So I looked over at her and asked, "Is everything okay?"

And the floodgates opened. She shared a struggle she was going through, why she was on the plane so late, and about her son, whom she was going to see and needed her help, and the story went on.

I listened, I listened, and I listened. I assured her I would be praying for her and appreciated her sharing her story with me.

And then she asked, "What about you? Where are you headed?"

Because I was prepared, because I was ready, even though I was *not willing* at this moment, the Holy Spirit took over, and I shared with her where I had been, what I had been doing, and now I was heading home.

Then I took the chance to ask her a simple question, turning the conversation from the physical to the spiritual, "Do you go to church anywhere?"

She shared with me a bit of her faith background and the journey she had been on. From what I could tell, she for sure knew a little about God but certainly had a lot of questions to be answered.

I had my iPad with me, so I asked her if I could share with her the best news the Bible has to tell everyone. Initially, I thought she would say "no," but to my surprise, she said "yes." So I opened up my Bible to a gospel app called "Share Your Faith."[20] (This app uses the bridge illustration to share the gospel with others clearly.)

I walked her through the app step-by-step, sharing the gospel, and at the end, it asks you to choose where you are on this faith journey using the bridge illustration. She indicated she was still on the side separated from God. At that point, I asked her if she thought she was ready to be on the other side, reunited with God through Jesus Christ as her Lord. I expected her to say "no," or "not right now," or "let me think about that." But without hesitation, she looked at me and said, "Yes, I want Jesus to be my King."

My jaw dropped, my eyes opened wide, and I said, "Right now?"

And she said, "Yes, right now; I'm ready." So, at 30,000 feet up, somewhere between Atlanta, Georgia, and Dallas, Texas, this lady called out to Jesus and was born again!

For that moment, at that time, I was God's plan to get God's news about His Son and His love to this woman. Because I was ready and prepared, because the Holy Spirit took over, even though my flesh was unwilling, this lady's life was changed forever.

I share this story not to brag on myself, but too brag about God. I share this story to remind myself and to remind you: You are God's plan to reach your world. One person at a time, one life at a time, one conversation at a time, and sometimes, one plane ride at a time! Salvation is the work of the Holy Spirit. Sharing His Word is the work of every Christian. God has a plan to reach people with the Good News of Jesus; ***that plan is you***!

#LiveSent Reflections: Take 5 minutes to answer these questions below.

1. What did the Holy Spirit say to you, and what stood out to you the most?
2. What scripture came to mind or spoke the loudest to you as you read?
3. What is one next step you can take today in light of what you just read?
4. Who do you know that needs to hear what you just learned about in this chapter?

#LiveSent Challenge: Find a simple app (Share Your Faith, Life in 6 Words, The God Text) from our resources page (see below) and put it on your phone so you can use it when the door opens.

To find out more about the Share Your Faith app and other great digital evangelism resources, check out our recourse page at: rageministries.com/resources.

CHAPTER 7

"Practice Makes________!"

"Also I heard the voice of the Lord, saying, 'Whom shall I send, and who will go for us?'"

"Then said I, 'Here am I; send me.'"

Isaiah 6:8

"We plan for so many less important things; why not plan for our evangelism?"

–Mark Dever

How'd He Get So Good?

Have you ever watched Steph Curry play basketball? This guy is amazing. Many experts say he is easily the best shooter the NBA has ever seen. Steph makes every shot look so easy.

Steph Curry is one of the best basketball players in the world. But how did he get so good? How is it that he makes every shot look like a layup? One word, *practice*. Steph Curry has been practicing his shooting since he was a little kid. His father, Dell Curry, was a professional basketball player, and he would often take Steph to the gym to practice. Steph would spend hours shooting, and he slowly developed into one of the best shooters in the world. Now, Steph is known for his incredible shooting ability, and it's all thanks to his practice. This truth remains: if you want to be good at something, remember: *practice* makes all the difference!

One of the best ways for you and me to get ready to share the gospel with others is to practice sharing the gospel. Here's what we know: *practice does not make perfect, but practice does make better.* In other words, that which we practice, what we repeat over and over again, we get better at. And when it comes to talking to other people about Jesus, you may be pleasantly surprised to find that when you practice, you'll begin making progress. So let me share with you a few tips on how to practice sharing your faith with others.

Family and Friends in the Faith

Start with those you know who already know Jesus. Find a trusted family member, friend, someone in your small group, or a Christian in your school club. Let them know you are trying to get better at sharing Jesus with others, and ask them if you can practice sharing the gospel with them. Ask them if they would give you an opportunity to take five minutes of their time. Ask them to listen and then give you honest and constructive feedback.

Starting with someone who already knows Jesus is crucial. Since this person is already a follower of Jesus, they can help you spot and clear up any theological confusion. A trusted friend can also help you sharpen your presentation where needed.

Once you have gotten a good flow and feel more confident and competent, I would move on to a friend or family member who doesn't know Jesus but has a good relationship with you. It is here that an awesome thing takes place. You have the opportunity to both practice sharing the gospel in a non-threatening way and can actually share the gospel with them in a non-threatening way. So identify a family member or find a friend you aren't sure knows Jesus as Lord, and practice sharing the gospel with them. You never know what God might do through this simple "practice."

Get Your Phone Out

Another incredible way to practice sharing Jesus with others is to record yourself sharing the gospel. Most of us have these amazing devices in our hands and at our disposal at all times: our phones. Every one of our phones has a camera. I would encourage you to take time to use your camera and record yourself sharing the gospel.

Now, this will probably be painful at first, maybe even a bit awkward, but I promise you it will be worth it. When you record yourself sharing the gospel, you will see the faces you make, any twitches you have, and you'll see what other people see when they hear you.

Do you play with your thumbs when you talk to them about Jesus? Do you smack, blink your eyes too much, or over-animate? You can see all this if you simply record yourself sharing the gospel. I promise you; if it's annoying to you, it's annoying to others. If it's distracting to you, it's distracting to others.

I recall the first time I actually watched a sermon I had preached. Though I had preached for a few years by that time, I had never actually watched or listened to one of my sermons. When I watched the sermon, honestly, it was painful. I had no idea how much I paced back and forth. I didn't realize how many times I used the word "man." I was totally oblivious to the number of times I said, "umm..."

Recording yourself gives you the opportunity to get better. It also allows you to share that recording with other believers for feedback.

Look at Yourself

If recording yourself is too painful, then try this. Practice sharing the gospel in front of a mirror. That's right, look at yourself in a mirror and talk to yourself about Jesus. Share the gospel with yourself.

Go through the outline with yourself. Practice sharing verses with yourself like you would anyone in need of Jesus. Look in the mirror; look yourself in the eye. Practice clear, concise communication.

When you do this in a mirror, you'll pick up all of your little intricacies that make sharing the gospel either better or it makes them worse. Take note and make necessary adjustments that help you share Jesus with others more clearly and concisely.

Tools Can Be a BIG Help

Have you ever tried to pull a nail out of the wall with your bare hands? Sometimes, you can yank it right out. Other times, though, it is impossible. So you grab a hammer, and boom, it comes out so easily. In that situation, you had the right tool for the job.

Sharing the gospel can be like that, too. Sometimes it will flow with ease in a simple conversation. At other times, you will need a tool to help you navigate the experience. I want to encourage you to find a simple gospel-sharing tool and practice it.

I wear a wristband almost everywhere I go. This wristband has the four emojis I shared with you in the previous chapter on it. They remind me of the four parts of the gospel conversation. They also serve as visual reinforcement as I am sharing as well. I can literally take this wristband and share the gospel with anyone, anywhere, at any time because I have practiced!

It certainly is not the only way … but it is a good way. Find a simple tool that you can have easily accessible when you are in a Jesus conversation. The wristband I wear has actually helped start a lot of conversations about Jesus. If you would like to order some of these wristbands for yourself, your group, or your church, we have these gospel wristbands available at www.wearerage.com.

Know Your Story

Finally, I would encourage you to know your testimony. While I will not go into the full training about this, sharing your testimony can be a great way to share the gospel. The simple flow of your testimony could follow this outline:

1. What was your life like before Christ?
2. When did you meet Jesus as Lord?
3. What Did Jesus change in you?
4. What is He doing recently?

Remember, we're not going for just gospel presentations; we want Jesus conversations. Conversations where we can share Jesus with others and give them a chance to trust Him as Lord. We want to be able to talk with people where they are about the God we know. And a lot of times, people love hearing stories. There is something powerful about a story. There is power in your story.

My Story Is Summarized like This …

I grew up in church. I knew about Jesus for most of my life that I could remember. At 18, I realized I knew a lot about Jesus but did not have a relationship with Him. I confessed Christ as my Lord, and He saved me that day. The moment He saved me, I felt called to the ministry. I knew that God was completely changing the outlook and the destination of my life. Since then, I've been able to preach the gospel across the globe, both in person and virtually. I've also been able to see thousands upon thousands come to know Jesus Christ as their Lord and Savior. God has provided and continues to open up doors each and every day of my life. And recently, He has given me an intense passion for sharing with others how they can share Jesus with others, which is why I'm writing this book.

No matter what your testimony is, I promise you God can and will use it. You just have to start sharing it.

If you practice sharing the gospel, you will be more competent, confident, and consistent in having Jesus conversations where you are, with who you know! Practice may not make perfect, but practice does make *better*. The more you practice, the better you will become at telling others about Jesus. You will get more confident, competent, and consistent. And that's a good thing because people need to hear about Jesus from His followers all the time—not every once in a while. So start practicing today! And if you ever find yourself struggling or doubting, remember this: God never gives up on us. So keep practicing and trusting Him; He has amazing things in store for you.

#LiveSent Reflections: Take 5 minutes to answer these questions below.

1. What did the Holy Spirit say to you, and what stood out to you the most?
2. What scripture came to mind or spoke the loudest to you as you read?
3. What is one next step you can take today in light of what you just read?
4. Who do you know that needs to hear what you just learned about in this chapter?

#LiveSent Challenge: Choose one way to practice sharing the gospel this week. If you choose to video it, our team would love to see it. Drop us a DM on IG or FB and share it with us (find us on any social media platform by searching #wearerage).

CHAPTER 8

You've Got to Start Somewhere, So Start Here

"The first thing Andrew did was to find his brother Simon and tell him, 'We have found the Messiah (that is, the Christ).' And he brought him to Jesus."

John 1:41–42, NIV84

"The question is not if God wants you involved in His mission, but where and how."

–J. D. Greear

One of the beautiful things about the gospel, the Good News of Jesus Christ, is that anyone, anywhere, at any time, who wants to be saved can … be … saved. Jesus said, "Whoever wants to come after me, let him…"[21] The want is where it begins. If you want Jesus, the great news is, you … can … have … Jesus.

So that begs the question, who are the people that we need to be telling about Jesus? Who are the people that you and I should be opening up our mouths and talking to about Christ? We see a really great pattern to follow when it comes to telling people about Jesus, and it all has to do with your circles. Your circles of influence. The circles of people in your life. And so, let's begin by identifying those in the circles of your life.

#LiveSent Starts with Your Circle

In Acts, Jesus teaches His disciples how the gospel will be spread. "*But you will receive power when the Holy Spirit comes on you; and you will be my witnesses in Jerusalem, and in all Judea and Samaria, and to the ends of the earth*" (Acts 1:8,

NIV84). Here's the pattern: Jerusalem (where they were), Judea (the surrounding area), Samaria (those outside their area), and the ends of the earth (everyone else).

So when you think of the people you need to first and foremost be sharing Jesus with, it is your immediate family. Start where you are, with who you know. This would be those individuals in your home—your mom, dad, and siblings. These would be people who are immediately and closely related to you.

If we are going to share the gospel, if we are going to #LiveSent, we must begin with those who are closest to us. Oh yes, I know. Those are the ones who know us best. Those are the ones who know our best sides and our worst sides. Yes, these are the people who will know and ought to have seen the change in your life.

But as you think about living sent, I want you to think about beginning right where you are with who you know. In Acts, there's a story recorded of Paul being in prison.[22] After God causes a great earthquake, the jailor discovers Paul is still there and has not escaped, so he asks, "What must I do to be saved?"

Paul replied, "Repent and believe, and you and your household will be saved."

What we see here is the intended working out of the gospel: we believe, we confess, we trust Jesus as Lord. Then those immediately closest to us would hear, see, and believe as well. So I want you to begin in your house.

After your inner circle, when you think about walking out this #LiveSent life, I want you to begin identifying your friends. Your coworkers. Your classmates. Your teammates. Those who are in your immediate realm of influence. Those who you do life with each and every day. Again, I would think about those in your school, those on your ball team, those who are with you, who see you week in and week out.

The Ripple Effect

I am reminded of the story of Stephen and Michael. Michael was a young man who had found Christ. He had come to know Jesus. The Lord had gotten a hold of his heart like never before, and Michael had a friend named Stephen, and Stephen took notice. Stephen began to notice the change in Michael's life, in his behavior, in his conversations, and in how Michael treated other people.

One day, Stephen asked, "Michael, what has happened to you?"

So, Michael began telling Stephen about Jesus. Little did Michael know this was an opportunity; Stephen was searching. He was looking. And he was in a crisis of belief in his life. And because he saw the life that Michael lived, and he heard the gospel that changed Michael's life, Stephen too turned and gave his life to Jesus Christ.

This is just one example of the power of our life, the power of our circle of influences. We must choose to "live sent." It all begins with our house, those directly in relationship with us, then moving to our friends, peer realm, coworkers, classmates, schoolmates, and teammates. Then I would say it moves into your neighborhood. It moves into your city and your community.

Think about it as waves rippling out from where a rock hits the water. The gospel hits your life. Hits your heart. And the effects of the gospel ripple out from there. We have family coming to Jesus, and friends coming to Jesus. Now neighbors and people in our community are coming to Christ. Why? Because the gospel changed us. Now we have the opportunity to share that news with others as well.

After your inner and outer circles, let me challenge you to think about your social media, online friends, and realms of influence. Now you may not see yourself as a social media influencer, but every one of you has an influence on people who see your online information. This is one of the easiest ways for you and me to let people know about our faith, by simple, clean posts on our social media.

Who are the people on your social media that you know do not know Jesus? Would you specifically begin praying for them and ask God to use some of your posts about your faith to resonate with them? I'm always amazed at messages I get from people who ask me about a post I made or comment on something I've shared about my faith. You never know how God can use a simple video, verse, or even picture. Ask God to help you leverage your social media in a way that makes much of Jesus and points people to Him.

Charles Spurgeon would write these convicting words many years ago, "Every Christian is either a missionary or an imposter." For the follower of Jesus, your very life is a mission trip. Everywhere we go, we are on mission.

So, we want to make sure that when we are walking out this #LiveSent life, we use these circles. Our family. Our friends. Our neighborhood. People that we know, right where we are. Then we move to the national and the global level. I don't believe we start going and telling by going on a mission trip. I don't believe that's where it starts. I believe it starts at home; then it goes overseas.

Remember what Jesus said: "You will be my witnesses in Jerusalem, Judea, Samaria, to the ends of the Earth." Home, friends, neighborhood, world. This is how the gospel begins to spread. We must be willing to walk across the street before we decide to go across the seas. So where do we begin this "live sent" life? We begin where we are, with who we know, right now.

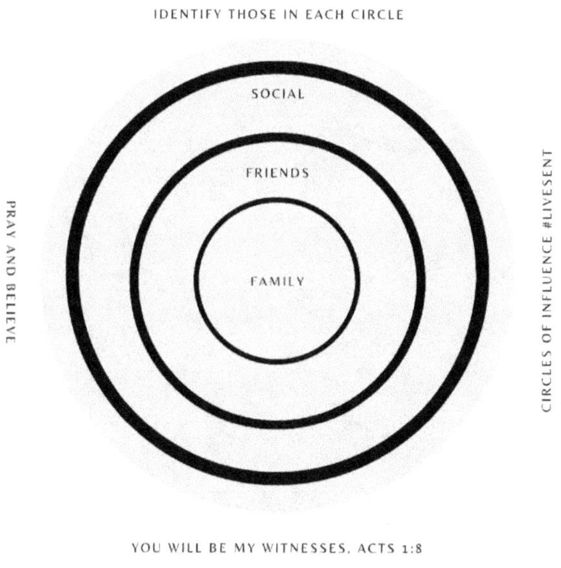

IDENTIFY THOSE IN EACH CIRCLE

SOCIAL

FRIENDS

FAMILY

PRAY AND BELIEVE

CIRCLES OF INFLUENCE #LIVESENT

YOU WILL BE MY WITNESSES, ACTS 1:8

#LiveSent Reflections: Take 5 minutes to answer these questions below.

1. What did the Holy Spirit say to you, and what stood out to you the most?
2. What scripture came to mind or spoke the loudest to you as you read?
3. What is one next step you can take today in light of what you just read?
4. Who do you know that needs to hear what you just learned about in this chapter?

#LiveSent Challenge: Download the Circles of Influence map at www.rageministries.com/resources, or use the one within this chapter and begin making an intentional prayer list of those in your realms of influence that need to hear about Jesus from you.

CHAPTER 9

Every Day Is Show and Tell Day

"Live such good lives among the pagans that, though they accuse you of doing wrong, they may see your good deeds and glorify God on the day he visits us."

1 Peter 2:12

"God forbid that I travel with anyone a quarter of an hour with anyone without speaking of Christ to them."

–George Whitefield

It has been said that the greatest single cause of atheism in the world today is Christians, who acknowledge Jesus with their lips and walk out the door and deny Him through their lifestyle.[23] If you and I want to be consistent in sharing the gospel with those around us, we need to be consistent in *living* the gospel out in front of others.

We all know that "people do not care what you have to say until they know that you truly care."[24] Every day, you and I have a chance, an opportunity to display the love of Jesus, give a chance to show that Jesus is not just some story in a book that's over 2000 years old, but rather, He is alive in our lives, working in us, working on us and working through us. So let me tell you real quickly how you and I can live a life that displays Jesus so that we can open up our mouths and declare Jesus. Let's begin with a story.

It's the story Jesus told when asked one day, "Who is my neighbor?" Instead of Jesus saying, "Well, everyone you come in contact with has the potential to be your neighbor," He told a story. It's the parable of the good Samaritan.[25]

In this story, Jesus shares about three men who encountered a man in need of help. This man had taken a trip and was robbed. He was beaten down. He was stripped. He was left half dead on the side of the road and was in desperate need of help.

Jesus tells the story of a priest who came by and saw the man but did nothing. Then a temple worker, a church employee, perhaps a youth pastor or a deacon, came by, saw the man, and once again, he did nothing. This, I believe, is how so many of us live our lives: busy, afraid, and blissfully unaware of those around us in need.

But then the story takes a twist, a turn … a Samaritan, a *nobody*, someone the world least expected to be the example; Jesus uses this man. The Bible says that when he saw the man, he had compassion on him. The Bible tells us further; he went to the man, bound up his wounds, poured on oil and wine, put him on his own donkey, took him to an inn, took care of him, and then made sure the bill was paid in full.

Live with Open Eyes

Now, in this story, there are some very clear examples that you and I can mark in our own life to walk out every single day. Number one, the Samaritan SAW THE MAN. If we are going to live a life that displays Jesus in our everyday life, we have to ask God to *give us eyes to see others around us.*

Unlike that of the priest and the temple worker, we have to ask the Lord to give us eyes, to see people in need, not to see them as a bother, not to see them as a pain, not to see them as a distraction, but rather to see them *as Jesus sees them.* See them as someone who needs Jesus—needs help, healing, and hope.

Reinhard Bonnke wrote this powerful truth about seeing others: "It is not that the Church hasn't been trained in evangelism; it is not a lack of instruction or information. The fact is, if you don't love people *through the eyes of Christ*, the world will never be changed." He is correct. If we do not ask God to give us His eyes for others, it will not matter how well-trained we are to share the gospel.

And so Jesus shares the story of the Samaritan. When he saw the man, he had compassion; he was so moved on the inside that he had to move on the outside. Therefore, we must pray, "Lord, help us see people as you see them, give us not merely physical sight but spiritual empathy, and help us sense where people are to understand their life." We need the Lord to get into our heads and hearts the truth of where people are because if we don't see as Jesus sees, we will never move or live as Jesus lived.

Serve with Compassion

Think about when Jesus saw the crowds. One day, He was going through the city and villages, healing, teaching, and preaching, then He saw the crowds. The Bible says He had compassion. Pastor Brandon Thomas shared recently, " Compassion is the highway on which God's grace is delivered to a world in need." You and I need to pray to *see with eyes full of compassion.*

Additionally, the Samaritan didn't only see the man; He *served* the man. If you and I are going to display Jesus in a world in desperate need of Him, we must not simply see their need; we have to serve the need. As David Livingstone wrote, "Sympathy is no substitute for action." This Samaritan did that: he went to the man, stooped down, cleaned him up, and used what he had to serve the other man. This is an example of *action*—doing something.

We all have resources. I understand all of our resources are different, but we all have resources. We all have something we can give. We all have something we can use. We all have something to serve with. For some of us, we don't have a lot of money, but we have a lot of time for others. We might not have as much time, but we have money. Some of us don't have many capabilities, but we have availability. And that is what the Lord is looking for. He's not looking for your capabilities. He's looking for your availability. You and I are called to help those Jesus brings into our lives.

Think about that for a second. If you're reading this book, you will encounter someone today that I, Ryan, who's writing this book, may never encounter. So it can't be my job to see them and serve them. It is your job. It is your opportunity. It is your chance to show Jesus to the person that Jesus has put into your life. Are you willing to do that? To stop and serve others in their time of need? Billy Graham reminded us, "God has given us two hands, one to receive with and the other to give with." Leverage what you have to do what you can where you are.

Go the Extra Mile

So this Samaritan first *saw* the man. Second, he *served* the man. Then, third, and lastly, he *sacrificed* for the man. Now, this is where most of us stop. We do not go the extra mile. We do not give until it hurts. We see and serve but do not ever sacrifice. But this is where we actually truly display Jesus; it is in the sacrifice.

When you and I see someone broke down on the side of the road; we may stop and help. We may make a call. We may do a little, but when we go the extra mile, take the next step, and sacrifice, we not only serve. When we give beyond what is expected—someone said it like this—we give until it hurts. Give until it costs you. Costs you time. Costs you money. Costs you a rearranging of your schedule.

Just the other day, my vehicle broke down on the side of the road. Water was shooting out of the engine; I had no idea what was happening. I quickly shot a video and sent it to a friend that I knew was a mechanic. I only asked him what was happening and where I should take it.

Immediately, my friend called me back. He told me exactly what was happening. He then instructed me to have the vehicle towed to his garage. He told me it might be a few days, but they would get it fixed. *Thank you, Jesus.* But he was not done.

By the time we got home, my friend let me know the parts were already on their way to his shop for my car. *That is awesome,* I thought. I was still thinking it would be a few days. To my surprise, though, he called me in just a couple of hours and asked if I could come to his house in an hour to get my vehicle. It was already done!

I could not believe it. When I got there, I asked him how he wanted payment. To my complete surprise, he said it was already "paid in full." He covered the cost! *What!?* I could not believe this. Not only had he fixed my car immediately, but he covered all the parts and labor! It cost me nothing.

All I had asked for was a recommendation and a little expert advice. My friend could have simply answered my question and helped me immensely. But he decided to go the "extra mile." He went above and beyond. He sacrificed his time, money, expertise, and resources for my benefit.

Most of us don't mind a little serving, a little giving, a little helping. But what happens when we rearrange our schedule? When we change our plans, when, for the sake of others, we say "no" to something we want, so others can have what they need?

You see, this is where the true display of Jesus comes out. Jesus sacrificed. Jesus laid it all down. Jesus paid the price. Jesus went the extra mile. Jesus loved beyond what was expected. Jesus humbled Himself. Jesus stooped down. Jesus took our cross. Jesus paid for our sins. Jesus owed us nothing yet gave us everything.

When you live a life of sacrifice and consistently display this to others, it is not all about you. They will truly begin seeing Jesus in us. In these moments, we are walking out the #LiveSent life.

If we want to show Jesus in a world that is losing its faith in Jesus, if we want to be able to open up our mouths and share with others about Christ, let us first open up our lives and display Christ on the daily. Ask the Lord, "Give me eyes to see, give me hands to serve, and give me a willingness to sacrifice so that others may see Jesus in order that they may be more willing to *hear* about Jesus."

#LiveSent Reflections: Take 5 minutes to answer these questions below.

1. What did the Holy Spirit say to you, and what stood out to you the most?
2. What scripture came to mind or spoke the loudest to you as you read?
3. What is one next step you can take today in light of what you just read?
4. Who do you know that needs to hear what you just learned about in this chapter?

#LiveSent Challenge: Take time this week to ask God about specific areas of your life that are not reflecting Him to others. Pray for the Holy Spirit to empower you to live a life that would open doors to share Jesus with others.

CHAPTER 1⊘

The Middle School Dance and Sharing the Gospel

When a Samaritan woman came to draw water, Jesus said to her, "Will you give me a drink?"

John 4:7

"Most Christians recognize the Importance of evangelism, but they are at a loss when it comes to striking up a conversation with a stranger on a plane, and a grocery line, or at the gas station."

–Matt Queen

There is an old saying attributed to St. Francis of Assisi. Many have debated if he really ever said this, but nonetheless, it is a popular slogan many Christians like. Truth be told, there are even churches that have it plastered on their walls.

"Preach the gospel, and if necessary, use words."

Now, at first glance, this may seem good. And if we are honest, this statement is a relief for many of us. Do you mean we can actually obey the command of Jesus to preach the gospel and not have to use any words?

Jesus said, "Go into all the world and ***preach the gospel*** to every creature" (Mark 16:15). This is a clear commission for every follower of Jesus to actually open up their mouth and make Jesus known to those in their world. As we just covered in the previous chapter, our good deeds, good works, and everyday life should display Jesus. But they never will be sufficient enough to declare Jesus.

And this is precisely where many of us stop. We pray, plan, prepare, learn a good outline, craft our testimony, know the gospel, and try to live a good and godly life … yet we never take time to open our mouths to share the gospel with anyone. Quite simply, we cannot share the gospel without using words.

In this chapter, I want to equip you with some tips to help you have the conversation. Tips that, when applied, will make you more comfortable not just to show Jesus in your everyday actions, but share Jesus in your everyday conversations. Let's focus on four main areas of a gospel conversation:

1. Start the conversation.
2. Turn the conversation.
3. Have the conversation.
4. Close the conversation.

Start the Conversation

First, how does one even start a conversation about Jesus? I would say that all conversations are a conversation that ***can*** end up being about Jesus. When we live with a heart that desires to see people know about Jesus, we begin viewing every conversation as a potential conversation about the Good News.

The truth is, we have conversations each and every day. The conversation could be in person, face to face, over the phone, via FaceTime, text message, or even social media. We have conversations at the coffee shop, in the lunchroom, in hallways, in the locker room, at home, on the phone via text, at practice, and in the breakroom at work. Literally, our day is full of conversations. Having conversations is the easy part. But making those conversations *intentional* is the real first step in sharing the gospel. When God begins to help us see each conversation as a potential conversation about Jesus, things begin to change. Of course, this does not mean we will share or need to share the gospel in every conversation. What it means is that we should ask God to give us a sensitive Spirit in our daily conversations to where they can be about Jesus.

Here are three encouragements to help you start seeing any conversation as a potential Jesus conversation:

1. Pray for opportunities and for boldness. Jesus, Himself, was always strategic in His interactions with people, and we see this throughout the Gospels. He was sensitive to the leading of the Holy Spirit for who He spoke to and when. As you pray, ask God to open doors for conversation and give you wisdom on how to take advantage of those opportunities. Also, ask Him to give you boldness—remember that you are an ambassador for Jesus Christ (2 Corinthians 5:20).
2. Be prepared. We should always be ready to give an answer for the hope that we have (1 Peter 3:15). When we know how to share the gospel more clearly, we will share the gospel more consistently. So don't forget to stay prepared.
3. Lead with love. Jesus was full of compassion, and our interactions should reflect that same love. As we share the gospel, our goal should be to point people to Jesus, not just convince them of some

> set of beliefs. When our motivation is love, we will be better able to communicate the Good News in a compelling and attractive way (Mark 12:30–31).

When we see every conversation as a potential Jesus conversation, we will have more conversations about Jesus.

Turn the Conversation

Most of us remember the awkwardness of the Middle School dance: all the guys on one side of the room, all the girls on the other. The wide open dance floor separates them like a great ocean. The only thing keeping the dance from getting started is for someone to get up the nerve to ask the question, "Do you want to dance?"

Shifting a conversation from everyday topics to Jesus can sometimes seem like this. We know what we are to be about. We know what the person needs to hear. We even know it is our job to make the first move. But how do we turn the conversation from football, food, work, sickness, the weather, politics … to faith? Turning the conversation never happens by accident, so let's get prepared to be intentional.

One of the best ways I have found to turn a conversation is by asking leading questions. Jesus was the master at questions, inviting dialogue, and creating an opportunity to share the gospel. Asking questions also lets you get to know the person you're speaking with, making it more likely that they'll be receptive to what you have to say.

Here are some sample questions you might consider using:

1. Would you say you have a personal relationship with Jesus, or are you still in the process?
2. What do you think of Christians? And why?
3. What do you believe about God?
4. What do you think will be your greatest contribution in this life?
5. Is religion important to you?
6. When you have problems or questions, who do you turn to for help?
7. From what or whom do you draw the strength to endure a difficult situation?
8. When you pray, who do you pray to? Why?
9. What do you think happens after our life here?
10. What do you think it takes for a person to enter heaven?
11. What causes your greatest concern or stress?
12. What do you believe about the Bible? Have you ever read it for yourself? What did you think about what you read?
13. What do you believe about Jesus?
14. When do you feel close to God? When do you feel far away from Him?
15. How do you deal with regrets from your past?

Ask God to help you see natural openings in everyday conversations that you can use to steer the discussion towards the gospel and ask one of these leading questions. When we ask questions, we give people the opportunity to talk. And we get the opportunity to listen. As they talk and we listen, we can get a real sense of where they are spiritually and point them to hope in Jesus. The opportunities to share about Christ are everywhere every day. Let's begin to take steps to shift the conversation and see what God does.

Have the Conversation

Once you have turned the conversation from everyday life to spiritual things, what do we do next? How do we actually have a gospel conversation? In other words, how do we get to share the gospel? Here are a few ways you can move from a general spiritual conversation to an actual Jesus conversation.

Ask Permission

This is one of my favorite and least direct ways to get to share the gospel with people. As you are in a conversation, you might ask something like this, "Do you mind if I share with you how I have dealt with the thought of death in my life?" If talking to someone about fear, you could say, "Do you mind if I share with you how I have overcome fear in my life?"

Each of these questions above asks permission to share. In each of these cases, you can easily turn to sharing the gospel by using the four pictures learned in Chapter 5 (God, Sin, Jesus, Decision). When we know the gospel outline, we can weave it into our conversation about overcoming fear, dealing with death, the meaning of life, and more.

Asking permission is an important part of sharing the gospel. It shows respect for the person and gives them the opportunity to say "no." Asking permission also allows Jesus to work in the person's life. He may give them the courage to say "yes" or soften their heart to receive the gospel. Either way, asking permission is an important part of sharing the gospel.

Apologize

Right now, you may be thinking, "Apologize? For what?" The apology is one easy way to get to share the gospel with a friend or family member whom you have known for a long time but have never shared the gospel.

For example, let's say you are conversing with a friend. In this conversation, you are talking about something you are both into, such as music. The conversation is going great. Then you realize something: you all have talked about so many things in life, but you have never told them about the most important thing that has ever happened to you in your life. At that moment, you could easily turn the conversation with an apology.

This happened to me one day when I wanted to share the gospel with my biological dad. I had every other weekend visits with my dad growing up. During those weekends, we would talk about sports, work, school, and those types of things. But when I was in my early 20s, I realized that since I was saved at 18, I had never shared the gospel with my dad.

So one day, during a conversation, I said, "Dad, I need to apologize to you."

He said, "For what?"

"We have talked about a lot of stuff over the years. We've talked about football, Nascar, work, school, and all sorts of stuff. But I have never told you about the most important thing that ever happened to me in my life. Could I do that right now?"

At that moment, my dad said, "Sure." So for the next thirty minutes or so, I was able to share my testimony and the gospel with him like never before. Trust me, I was nervous, and it was not easy at all. But I got to tell my dad about Jesus, which is what mattered most.

I wonder who in your life you need to apologize to and ask for a chance to share Jesus with them?

All In

The last way I want to share with you about how to actually "have the gospel conversation" is to just go "all in." By this, I mean just start sharing Jesus with someone. You can do this in several ways, but let me just share a couple.

If you are in a conversation with someone and feel like there is a need for them to hear about Jesus, you could ask, "Do you mind if I share with you real quickly a story that changed my life?" With this one simple question, you are asking permission and setting up for an easy presentation of the gospel.

I really have used that question to share the gospel with family, friends, and total strangers. I have used it to have 30-minute talks and also share the gospel in 30 seconds with the person in the McDonald's drive-through window. I ask that question and then share the gospel with them using the four symbols learned in Chapter 5. If it's a quick conversation, I often give them the wristband I am wearing and let them know they can learn more at www.JesusSave.me, the website on the back of the wristband.

Another option, if the burden to share with someone comes on you, is to say, "I never will forget the day my life changed forever. Can I share that with you quickly?" Statements like that help grab people's attention and give you an opportunity to share your testimony and the gospel.

Again, I would remind you this is why it is so important to have a gospel flow memorized as well as have your testimony well known. It is in these moments that people are open to hearing your experience and the gospel.

Sometimes you just need to jump right in. Sometimes you know you can't wait another day or another moment. In these times, it is really good to have a transitional statement you are comfortable with that gets you permission to share Jesus.

Close the Conversation

So you got the chance to share the gospel with someone in a clear and concise way. What do you do next? How do we close, or end, the conversation with the person? I think there are two important things to keep in mind at this stage.

First, ask if what you have shared makes sense to them. By asking this question, you can see if there is anything you need to explain further or truths they may be struggling with. Take time here to be sensitive to where they are, and truly try and help them in any way you can.

If, at this moment, they ask you a question you cannot answer, tell them that. Let them know you would be happy to find that answer for them and meet up again. This gives a wonderful opportunity to continue the conversation at another time.

Second, if you sense you have answered all questions they have, simply ask, "Has there ever been a time when you gave your life to Christ as Lord and Savior?" It is here you get to know more about their story and where they are spiritually.

Often here, people will point to works. They will respond with something like, "Yes, I've been baptized," or "Yes, I am a pretty good person," or "Yes, I go to church when I can," or "Yes, my mom took me to church all the time," or even "Yes, I believe in God." While all of these things are good, none point to them trusting Jesus as Lord.

In these moments, I always give the person an opportunity to trust Jesus. I use one verse, Romans 10:9, and walk them through it. I show them how there is a call to confess Jesus as Lord and faith that God raised Him from the dead in order for them to be saved.

After sharing this, I ask them if they are ready to confess Jesus as Lord and invite Him to live in them as King forever. In doing this, I never try to force someone, but I certainly don't want to leave someone hanging out there who is ready to call on Christ, either. We want people to make a decision based on their own convictions, not because we pushed them into it!

Lastly, I close in one of two simple ways. If they trust in Christ, I celebrate with them and either invite them to church with me or, if I am in another place, I get their information to send them a book on what's next. Either way, I want to make sure they know what has happened and what steps they should be taking next.

If someone doesn't confess Christ, then I let them know I am praying for them. I make sure they know I love them and want to help them in any way I can. If it's a friend, I assure them I will be here for them and will be ready to talk whenever they are. If it's a stranger, I point them to our website, www.JesusSave.me, and encourage them to go there if they ever have more questions.

Two Big "What Ifs"

I have found we all have two fears before entering a conversation with someone about Jesus. "What if" they say "no" to the conversation, and "what if" they ask me a question I do not know. Let me give you a few simple ways I have personally found to help with those real-life realities.

When it comes to sharing Jesus, we need to know everyone will not always be open to hearing. Whether you are trying to share with a friend or a total stranger, sometimes they simply will tell you they don't want to hear about it. Here are a couple of reminders when this happens (and it happens to us all).

Do ...

1. Be loving: we are called to speak the truth in love.
2. Be respectful: we are told to answer others with gentleness and respect (Colossians 4:6).
3. Be courteous: tell the person something simple like, "Thank you anyway; I hope you have a great day."
4. Leave the door open: let them know, when they are ready to talk, you will be ready to share.

Don't ...

1. Be pushy: remember, we are not called to push but to share.
2. Be argumentative: our goal is not to win an argument, but love people and share the gospel.
3. Take it personally: people are not rejecting you, but Jesus.

When you enter into conversations about faith, you may encounter someone who has legitimate, tough questions. This is actually one fear that keeps many people from talking about Jesus. J. D. Payne offers a great reminder for those of us who feel we ought to be able to answer every question someone might have before we start sharing Jesus with them. Payne says, "God does not need you or me to be his bodyguard. He does not need us to be his defense. He is big enough to take care of himself. So when someone challenges you with a question you can't answer, don't freak out."

The fear of not knowing the answer to someone's tough question can be paralyzing. But it does not have to be. In these situations, I want to offer you some easy tips when faced with tough questions.

1. Know these questions may come. Knowing they may come will set your mind at ease and keep you from being taken aback by one.
2. If you know the answer, share the answer. Some of the questions people ask, you know the answer to. If you know it, share it in love.
3. If you don't know, tell them. If you don't know the answer, simply say something like, "That is a great question. I need to research that. Can we set a time for me to get back to you on what I find?" In the case of a family or friend who has questions, you may even invite them to research the answer with you.
4. Flip the script. You can sometimes flip the question back on them when asked a question. For example, if someone asked me, "Do you really think we were created?" I may simply say, "I do believe we were created. Where do you believe we came from?" Or "How do you believe it all

began?" Let them think about their own worldview and you will also gain more insight as to where they are coming from.

5. Remember, we don't have every answer. The truth is, none of us have all the answers to all the questions. Sometimes we just have to be okay with not knowing and simply trusting in faith.

Closing Reminders

As a Christian, you will feel led to talk to others about your faith. This can seem like a daunting task, but remember that you are not alone—the Holy Spirit will guide and equip you for this important work. Remember, it is our job to tell; it is God's job to save.

Sharing Jesus does not have to be scary. If you follow these simple steps in this chapter, you can easily turn any conversation into an opportunity to share the gospel. You never know what God might do through your simple act of sharing Jesus with someone else. I have found that the more Jesus conversations I have, the more Jesus conversions I see!

#LiveSent Reflections: Take 5 minutes to answer these questions below.

1. What did the Holy Spirit say to you, and what stood out to you the most?
2. What scripture came to mind or spoke the loudest to you as you read?

3. What is one next step you can take today in light of what you just read?
4. Who do you know that needs to hear what you just learned about in this chapter?

#LiveSent Challenge: Who is one person you can have the conversation with this week? Identify which way you will start the conversation with them and practice what you will say.

CHAPTER 11

Someone's Forever Depends on It

"I looked for someone among them who would build up the wall and stand before me in the gap on behalf of the land so I would not have to destroy it, but I found no one."

Ezekiel 22:30

"Could a mariner sit idle if he heard the drowning cry?
Could a doctor sit in comfort and just let his patients die?
Could a fireman sit idle, let men burn and give no hand?
Can you sit at ease in Zion with the world around you damned?"

–Leonard Ravenhill

Many of you right now may be wondering exactly what many Christians wonder, "Ryan, do I really need to tell other people about Jesus?" You may be thinking to yourself right now, "If God wants to save them, and if God desires to save them, then surely God can save them. Can't God do this all without me?"

The answer to this question is "no." God, in His sovereignty, has chosen a way to save people. God, in His sovereignty, has decided to use men and women like you and me to open up our mouths and tell others about Jesus. In the words of the late Hudson Taylor, we would do well to remember, "The Great Commission is not an option to be considered; it is a command to be obeyed."

One of my favorite promises in scripture is found in Romans chapter 10:13. Paul writes these words, "Whoever calls upon the name of the Lord will be saved." What a promise. I love that Paul clearly and succinctly states, "whoever." Yes, I would tell you right now, whoever wants to be saved can be saved.

And whoever wants to be saved and calls upon the name of the Lord **will be saved**. Romans 10:13 is a power-packed promise. But Paul does not stop there. The very next verse drops this reminder. Paul asks a series of questions. He says, "*How, then, can they call on the one they have not believed in? And how can they believe in the one of whom they have not heard? And how can they hear without someone preaching to them?*"[26]

He says in Romans 10:13, "Whoever calls upon the name of the Lord **will be saved**." Don't miss that. In order to be saved, someone must **call** on the name of the Lord. He immediately follows that up by saying that whoever calls needs to first **believe**. No one can call on someone that they haven't believed in.

And then he says, "Well, how will they ***believe*** unless they ***hear***? How will you believe someone you've never heard about?" And then he asks, "How will they ***hear*** if someone doesn't ***tell*** them?" Do you see it? It all hinges on you and me going and telling!

It goes like this …

If we don't ***tell***, people can't ***hear.***

If people ***don't*** hear, they can't ***believe.***

If people don't ***believe***, they can't ***call.***

If people don't ***call***, they can't be ***saved.***

My friend, do not miss this. People need to ***hear*** about Jesus in order to call on Jesus. And this is where you and I come in.

Go and Tell

So Paul says, "How can they hear unless someone tells them?" And then he says, "And how can they tell unless they are ***sent?***" Have you been sent? Yes. Over and over. We have been told by Jesus, "Go; go and tell, go make disciples, go preach the gospel, go as I have come, ***I'm sending you***. You will receive power when the Holy Spirit comes on you, and you will be my witnesses and Jerusalem, Judea Samaria into the other most parts of the earth."[27] That means no matter where you are, there are people where you are that need Jesus.

So will you go and tell in order for people to come to Christ? They must hear in order to believe; they must be told in order to tell, and we must be sent. And we all, as Christ-followers, have been sent.

May I remind you of the very first thing Jesus told James and John, "Come follow me, and I will make you become fishers of men"? Followers are fishers. Saved people are sent people.

As you read these words on this page, know that if the Lord has saved you, He has sent you. If the Lord has called you to follow Him, He has called you to fish for men.

So today, don't doubt God's plan in your life. He wants you to tell others about Jesus. When you and I choose to tell, that gives people an opportunity to hear. When people hear, they can believe. When they believe they can call. When they call on Jesus as Lord, they are saved.

We are called to live a life that is serious about telling others about Jesus. If we don't tell them, they will never hear. And if they never hear, how can they believe? If they don't believe, how can they call on Jesus as Lord and be saved?

It is up to us to share the gospel with the world so that all may come to know Him. Let's not take this task lightly but instead commit ourselves fully to reaching those who are lost. God has called us to do this work. Let's answer His call.

Lord, are you looking for one still?
I'll be one who will #LiveSent.

#LiveSent Reflections: Take 5 minutes to answer these questions below.

1. What did the Holy Spirit say to you, and what stood out to you the most?
2. What scripture came to mind or spoke the loudest to you as you read?
3. What is one next step you can take today in light of what you just read?
4. Who do you know that needs to hear what you just learned about in this chapter?

#LiveSent Challenge: Identify one person on your prayer list with whom you will share the gospel this week. Set the time and start the conversation.

CHAPTER 12

Where Do We Go from Here?

"Do not merely listen to the word, and so deceive yourselves. Do what it says."

James 1:22

"It wouldn't matter if Jesus died 1000 times if no one ever hears about it."

–Martin Luther

Practical Next Steps

After a powerful encounter with the Lord, Isaiah heard these words, "Whom shall I send? And who will go for us?" In response to this question, Isaiah answered, "Here am I. Send me!"[28]

As you have walked through this book, I have no doubt the Holy Spirit of God has been prompting you to go and tell your world about Jesus. I have no doubt you, like Isaiah, have a desire in your heart that is saying, "Here I am. Send me."

Why will some read this book and begin sharing their faith while others will remain the same? The answer is simple: it's not a lack of information for many of us; it's a lack of execution. You may know what you need to do, but if you don't take action, nothing will change.

So often, we read a book or attend a seminar, and we're filled with motivation and excitement to make changes in our lives. But then, we go back to our old habits and do nothing different. If you don't want that to happen in the realm of personal evangelism, you have to be intentional about putting what you've learned into action. I have heard it said, "It's not a lack of information for many of us; it's a lack of action."

In this book, I have given you a lot of information. For some, this information has all been brand new. For others, this was just a good refresher. The question now is, will you act upon the information you have been given? To help you get started, I want to close by giving you a few simple, actionable steps to begin taking so that you will truly #LiveSent.

#LiveSent Tip 1 – Record Your Story, The World Needs to Know

I want you to record yourself sharing your story. Don't worry if you don't have a lot of time or if it's not perfect. Just take two minutes and share your story. Once you have that recorded, post it on social media so others can be encouraged by your story. When we share our testimonies, we inspire others to do the same, and that is what will change the world.

A simple outline to follow would be:

1. My life before Christ: 30 seconds.
2. When did you meet Jesus: 30 seconds.
3. What did Jesus change in you: 30 seconds.
4. What is He doing now: 30 seconds.

So, go out and make a video. It doesn't have to be perfect. In fact, the more real you are, the better it will be. And don't forget to share it with your family and friends. Ask them what they think about your story and if they have one like it. Who knows? You might just start a Jesus conversation with them.

#LiveSent Tip 2 – Make a Prayer Wall, We All Need Reminders

Prayer is one of the most powerful weapons we have in our spiritual arsenal, and when used correctly, it can change not only our lives but also the lives of those around us. Take some time to read through the "7 #LiveSent Prayers" listed in Chapter 3 and incorporate them into your daily prayers. Find a place where you can put the list of names of people you are praying for so that you can keep them top-of-mind. And don't forget to ask God to help you become more effective at gospel conversations in your everyday life.

#LiveSent Tip 3 – Get a Partner, Two Are Better Than One

When it comes to the race of life, we all need someone to run with us. We were not made to walk alone, and when we have people in our lives who will help us and encourage us, we are able to accomplish more. So find someone you can partner with and keep each other going in this daily call to share Jesus in this world.

#LiveSent Tip 4 – Start Now, Delayed Obedience Is Disobedience

Don't wait until you are "ready." The truth is, you will never be fully ready. There will always be more to learn. There will always be another question to answer. There will always be another person to tell. The best day to tell someone about Jesus is today! Start now; start today! You don't need a theology degree or perfect evangelism skills. Just start where you are with the people God has put in your life, and take one step forward each day. We would love to help you on your journey, so please don't hesitate to reach out for support!

#LiveSent Tip 5 – Pass It on to Someone Else and Be a Blessing

As you have read at the end of each chapter in this book, I believe you need to be passing on to others what God is teaching you. There is a true statement that says, "Evangelism is more caught than taught." One of the best ways to continue to grow in your personal witness is to bring someone alongside you. So find someone you can pass what you are learning and practicing on to each week. Who will it be? Will you take some time this week to prayerfully consider who that might be? Let's get started!

#LiveSent Tip 6 – Celebrate Every Win

Every seed planted is a step closer to someone coming to Jesus. Don't forget to celebrate. Celebrate every post, every conversation, every attempt to share the gospel. It may not seem like much, but it is a seed planted. So let's celebrate every small win along the way! What gets celebrated gets replicated. When we remember that even one person hearing about Christ is cause for great celebration, it helps us to keep going when things get tough. And don't forget—we only fail if we don't tell. So share your story with someone today and rejoice in the victory!

#LiveSent Tip 7 – Follow and Tag Us Up

At R.A.G.E. Ministries, we are always posting ideas, tips, and stories of how we can share the gospel with confidence, competence, and consistency. If you are on social media, we'd love for you to follow us so you can stay encouraged. Also, we hope you'll take a few minutes to share what God is doing in and through your life with us on social media. When we see and celebrate what God is up to, it encourages us all—so make sure to tag our account so we can join the party! And if you have any ideas you think would encourage others, please pass them along. We love hearing from you and being part of encouraging others as they follow Jesus. What has God been doing in your life lately?

You can find us on all social media by searching: #wearerage.

Thank You for Reading *Live Sent!*

I'm so glad you decided to pick up this book and learn more about how to #LiveSent. If you enjoyed this book and gained confidence in sharing Christ, I'd love to hear about your experiences! And if you'd like to encourage others to pick up this book, head over to Amazon and leave a review to share your journey so others can #LiveSent.

Thank You!

LET'S CONNECT

Email: office@rageministries.com
Website: www.rageministries.com.
Social media: #wearerage

Find us on YouTube: RAGEMinistries

Together "We Are R.A.G.E."
Ryan Fontenot

About the Author

Ryan Fontenot is the Founder and Lead Communicator for R.A.G.E. Ministries (www.rageministries.com). R.A.G.E. (Reaching A Generation Endangered) exists to PROCLAIM the gospel of Jesus and to PREPARE the next generation to do the same.

Since 2003, Ryan has spoken to hundreds of thousands across North America and around the globe. With a gift of passionate and creative preaching, God is using Ryan to point this generation to Jesus.

We partner with churches, camps, conferences, conventions, and Christians everywhere in proclaiming the life-changing gospel of Jesus and equipping the next generation in declaring the gospel.

For additional resources, information on having Ryan come to speak at your next event or to financially support R.A.G.E. Ministries, visit: www.rageministries.com.

May we work together to mobilize the mission of Reaching A Generation Endangered.

Together "We Are R.A.G.E."

R.A.G.E. MINISTRIES
P.O. Box 80417
Keller, TX 76248
office@rageministries.com
www.rageministries.com

Notes

Chapter 1

Conrad Hackett and David McClendon, "Christians Remain World's Largest Religious Group, but They Are Declining in Europe," Pew Research Center (Pew Research Center, May 31, 2020), https://www.pewresearch.org/fact-tank/2017/04/05/christians-remain-worlds-largest-religious-group-but-they-are-declining-in-europe/.

2 "World Population Prospects - Population Division," United Nations (United Nations, August 15, 2020), https://population.un.org/wpp/DataQuery/.

3 Daniel A. Cox and Karlyn Bowman, "Generation Z and the Future of Faith in America," The Survey Center on American Life, April 4, 2022, https://www.americansurvey-center.org/research/generation-z-future-of-faith/.

4 "Global Report," *Global Youth Culture,* OneHope, (2020): 4. https://onehope.net/wp-content/uploads/2020/10/Global-Youth-Culture-1.pdf.

5 "Global Report," *Global Youth Culture,* OneHope, (2020): 7. https://onehope.net/wp-content/uploads/2020/10/Global-Youth-Culture-1.pdf.

6 "Global Report," *Global Youth Culture,* OneHope, (2020): 12. https://onehope.net/wp-content/uploads/2020/10/Global-Youth-Culture-1.pdf.

7 "Global Report," *Global Youth Culture,* OneHope, (2020): 14. https://onehope.net/wp-content/uploads/2020/10/Global-Youth-Culture-1.pdf.

8 “Global Report,” *Global Youth Culture,* OneHope, (2020). https://onehope.net/wp-content/uploads/2020/10/Global-Youth-Culture-1.pdf.

9 Lifeway Research, “Study: Churchgoers Believe in Sharing Faith, Most Never Do,” Lifeway Research, December 22, 2020, https://research.lifeway.com/2014/01/02/study-churchgoers-believe-in-sharing-faith-most-never-do/.

Chapter 2

10 Mark C. Perna, “The Why Gen: Meet Our next Greatest Generation,” Forbes (Forbes Magazine, October 22, 2019), https://www.forbes.com/sites/markcperna/2019/10/22/the-why-gen-meet-our-next-greatest-generation/?sh=3ab67fbd3ab8.

11 “Global Report,” *Global Youth Culture,* OneHope, (2020): 7. https://onehope.net/wp-content/uploads/2020/10/Global-Youth-Culture-1.pdf.

12 Pauline J. Chang, “Barna Survey: Evangelism Most Effective to Youth,” The Christian Post, October 13, 2004, https://www.christianpost.com/news/barna-survey-evangelism-most-effective-to-youth.html.

Chapter 3

13 Mark Batterson, *Circle Maker* (Zondervan, 2016).

14 Matthew 9:37; Luke 10:2.

Chapter 4

15 Rice Broocks, *Man, Myth, Messiah - Answering History's Greatest Question* (Thomas Nelson Publishers, 2016).

16 Romans 3:10; Romans 3:23; Romans 6:23a.

17 Romans 5:8; Romans 6:23b.

18 Romans 10:9–10; Romans 10:13.

19 2 Kings 7:8.

Chapter 6

20 "Share Your Faith App," Share Your Faith Ministries -, accessed October 13, 2022, https://howtoshareyourfaith.com/.

21 Matthew 16:24.

Chapter 8

22 Acts 16:26–33.

23 Quote from Brennan Manning , author of *The Ragamuffin Gospel.*

Chapter 9

24 Quote from Theodore Roosevelt.

25 Luke 10:25–37.

26 Romans 10:14.

Chapter 11

27 Acts 1:8.

Chapter 12

28 Isaiah 6:8.

www.ingramcontent.com/pod-product-compliance
Lightning Source LLC
LaVergne TN
LVHW010622100826
845148LV00014B/3072

9798887594972